Learning in
Denmark

1997 The Danish Cultural Institute, Copenhagen
Secretary-General: Finn Andersen

This publication was co-ordinated by Lisbeth Manicus,
head of the Job-Swop Programme

Editors:
Hanna Broadbridge, Ib Fischer Hansen and Peder Kjøgx
Translator: Edward Broadbridge
Illustrations: Morten Nilsson, RAGNAROK

Acknowledgement: Piet Hein © Illustrations & Grooks,
page 16, 88, 95, 107, 115 Reprinted with kind permission
of Piet Hein as, DK-Middelfart

Layout & Dtp: Forlaget Systime, Århus

Cover design: Carsten Lassen

Printed by Nørhaven A/S, Viborg

This book has been published with the support of the
Danish Ministry of Education, Danish Teachers Union
and Union of Danish High School Teachers

Printed in Denmark 1997
ISBN 87 7429 0924 Det Danske Kulturinstitut

Det Danske Kulturinstitut
Kultorvet 2
DK 1175 Copenhagen K
Tel. (+45) 33 13 54 48
E-mail: dancult@cultur.dk

Contents

Foreword

Per Himmelstrup

It is now generally accepted that the internationalisation of education at every level and by every means possible is absolutely essential.

The Danish Cultural Institute is contributing to this process through its Job-Swop programme, by which teachers from all sectors of the education system exchange schools with colleagues throughout the world. This ranges from direct exchange, in which a Danish and a foreign teacher swop jobs and homes for 2-3 weeks, to more study-oriented stays and even to temporary appointments of up to a year in length.

Through such an international programme teachers can learn a great deal about each other and about the various educational systems, methods and current ideas in the country in question. They gain first-hand experience, compare quality and styles, and discuss strengths and weaknesses. Finally, they are challenged to evaluate their own particular brand of teaching – by measuring themselves against others. Pupils also benefit indirectly by being confronted with a new "foreign" teacher and by new stimuli from their own returning teacher. Indeed, they may even derive concrete benefit through personal mail contact or, as in some cases, even a subsequent class or pupil exchange.

Among the methods that Danes seek to emphasize and stimulate throughout our system is the classroom conversation – the interactive dialogue among the pupils, as well as between pupils and teacher. The conversation as a teaching method has a long history in Denmark.

Much time is also spent discussing ethics, more so perhaps than religion.

Nevertheless, there is still widespread reluctance among teachers towards transferring specific values and norms directly onto the pupils. This can easily lead to a mild form of indoctrination. The influencing of attitudes must be done more indirectly, so pupils are encouraged to practise taking responsibility and trying to influence others in the classroom as well as in the institution in general.

Finally, in addition to their firm educational grounding pupils are encouraged to understand the need to continue to learn throughout their lives, whether inside or outside organised institutions of learning. Learning does not end with graduation from school or college.

Denmark enjoys a very long tradition of regarding the product of education as being a personal matter, hard to measure and grade. For while education is undeniably a national concern, it also aims at personal development and enrichment, the idea being that even learning for one's own sake is of benefit to the community.

In recent years serious questions have been asked of the Danish educational system, still regarded as among the best in the world. This book from the Danish Cultural Institute seeks to contribute to the debate and the international exchange of experience, as well as to acquaint our many visitors with the various ways and means of learning in Denmark.

1. The Plain Life –
Danish Culture and Mentality

Jørgen Carlsen

When Danes are asked by foreigners to point out something peculiar to the Danish mentality they often mention the Jante Law. With a shrug of the shoulders they say Denmark is governed by the Jante Law, and other Danes nod in reluctant agreement.

The Jante Law

The term itself was coined by the Danish-Norwegian writer, Aksel Sandemose, in his novel *A Fugitive Crosses his Tracks* (1933), where the law is applied by the petty-minded bourgeoisie of the fictional town of Jante to the glorification of all that is mediocre. For Sandemose, however, the town was more than fiction; he himself had experienced at first hand the claustrophobia of a medium-sized provincial Danish town in which deviation from the norm is a highly presumptuous, even a social sin. Among the 10 commandments of the Jante Law are:

> You must not believe you *are* anybody.
> You must not deceive yourself into thinking you are better than us.
> You must not believe you are more than us.

In Jante you are not expected to differ from the crowd, to achieve excellence in any field, to be gifted, talented or in any way out of the ordinary. You must be like the others.

The Jante Law is thus a modest characterisation of the Danes by the Danes, mediocrity being stamped on the Danish mentality and lifestyle. Nor is this a recent phenomenon; there is a centuries-old tradition of foreigners coming to Denmark and noting it as a national characteristic. Thus in *An Account of Denmark as It was in the Year 1692* the English diplomat Robert Molesworth, after 3 years as an envoy in Copenhagen, wrote:

"To conclude; I never knew any Country where the Minds of the People were more of one calibre and pitch than here; you shall meet with none of extraordinary Parts or Qualifications, or excellent in particular studies and Trades; you see no Enthusiasts, Mad-men, Natural Fools, or fanciful Folks, but a certain equality of understanding reigns among them; every one keeps the ordinary beaten road of Sence, which in this country is neither the fairest nor the foulest, without deviation to the right or left; yet I will add this one Remark to their praise, that the Common People do generally write and read."

It would seem at first sight that there is not much to shout about in Denmark. The Danes as a people are anything but exciting, let alone brilliant. There are very few geniuses: Hans Christian Andersen, H. C. Ørsted, Søren Kierkegaard, Niels Bohr and possibly a couple of others. But for Danes they are close to being the exceptions that prove the rule.

On the other hand the deeper point is that in the nature of the word a genius is a rare being. And Danes in general do not regard geniuses as superhuman, or even people in some way higher up the ladder. However outstanding a person may prove to be, they are neither more nor less than just another fellow human being; the Danish mentality tends towards seeking likenesses rather than differences.

Perhaps indeed the Jante Law is not even peculiar to Denmark. The great German philosopher Hegel may in an unguarded moment have said he saw "the spirit of the world on horseback" as he watched Napoleon ride into Jena in 1806, but he is also the author of the sober thought that "No man is a hero to his valet". This is down-to-earth wisdom; the closer we get to a person, the more human they become. It is the distance, the lack of acquaintance, that creates the mystique; close up even the greatest have more in common than in contrast. So the Jante Law may be Danish but the phenomenon is not confined to Denmark. A closer examination would doubtless reveal something similar in every society and culture.

Down-to-earth self-awareness

Nor should the foreigner be dazzled by the Danes' modesty. "Danes are world champions at hating themselves," says Hans Magnus Enzensberger, the German-Norwegian writer. Even if he is right, this is still only a half-truth. For though the Danes regularly refer to their Jante Law, there is no implication that Danish culture and national life are a lost cause. As the Danish historian Uffe Østergaard has said, "The Danes are without doubt the world's most modest people – here too they surpass all others." This paradox between demonstrative humility and discreet self-assertion contains more than a grain of truth, as many a foreign visitor can testify. Apparent Danish humility often turns out on closer inspection to rest on an impressive foundation of self-promotion. The conspicuous modesty thus serves to balance out the underlying self-satisfaction, which is in fact far more notable for its fundamental lack of modesty.

We might even go so far as to maintain that what characterises Danish culture is actually the opposite of the Jante Law.

The temptation is to call it the Jante Law stood on its head. The Jante Law has a dialectical flipside, so to speak, which turns what could be construed as negative into something positive. For it can also be read the other way up. When it tells people not to think they are something special, it is quite simply because being special is not something that individuals have a monopoly on. People are not a faceless mass, but a variegated array of individuals with no particular claim to being regarded as outstanding since every person in their very essence is important.

This striking self-awareness among so-called ordinary people can be traced back a long way in Danish cultural history, and is found in the folk wisdom of proverbs and sayings. At the end of the 17th century, as Robert Molesworth was writing down his views on the Danes, the theologian and educationalist Peder Syv (1631-1702) published a collection of these ancient proverbs, many with counterparts in other cultures, such as You cannot jump over your own shadow, A miaowing cat catches no mice, and Love without money does not last long. But now and again there are sayings which are typically Danish in content, such as A doctor and a peasant know more than a doctor alone.

The characteristic Danish element here is down-to-earthness: we are all walkers in our various walks of life walking around with both feet on the ground and something to tell each other. Of course the doctor is a clever man, but he is not too clever to learn from the simple peasant, who though he cannot read and write has his senses about him and a fund of experience to draw on. However skilled the doctor may be he will expand his horizon together with the peasant. Each can learn from the other.

The same motif is to be found in the Danish comedy, *Erasmus Montanus* (1723) by the philosopher-playwright, Ludvig Holberg (1684-1754), who can

best be described as a Danish blend of Molière and Voltaire. Erasmus, a conceited student, comes home to his birthplace and makes a fool of himself with his academic knowledge. Even though he is right to claim that the earth is round he comes a cropper at the hands of popular wisdom. The real fool is not the ignoramus but the intellectual who is deceived into thinking he understands the whole wide world but does not even understand himself. Erasmus is a fool because his learning has made him a stranger to himself, right down to his latinized name. For Erasmus Montanus was born Rasmus Hill. His inability to come down to earth prevents him from fulfilling his original purpose for returning home: to marry his childhood sweetheart Lisbeth. Not until the end of the play does he realize that in certain circumstances it is wisest to assume that the earth is as flat as a pancake and life is not worth sacrificing on the altar of theoretical speculation. The plain man's simple life has its own admirable virtues and respected qualities, living as he does with hope and disappointment, joys and sorrows.

In Hans Christian Andersen's story, *The Emperor's New Clothes*, we find the same theme of simple folk-wisdom triumphing over the masquerade of pretence at the royal court.

Because of intrigue and opportunism nobody dares to speak out, so two travelling apprentice tailors take advantage of the situation by sewing an invisible suit for the Emperor. Fearing their own exposure all the courtiers pretend to admire this splendid example of haute couture, until during the procession through town a little child spontaneously notes that the Emperor "has nothing on"! Only then is the silence broken and people admit to their experiences. Again the truth comes from someone without pretence, someone who is down-to-earth, a child of the people.

What shall we live for?

Even the philosopher Søren Kierkegaard circles round the same motif. Despite his often sophisticated and difficult thought, in the final analysis he is attempting to put a stop to pomposity, insincerity and pretence. He seeks a simple plainness for the people, even though he himself is far from being a down-to-earth philosopher. Reality must not be thought out of existence. In his attack on Hegel, who has built a magnificent philosophical castle for himself, Kierkegaard asks where does Hegel live. In the castle? No, in a little doghouse beside it. For there is no room for Hegel in his own thought. Commenting on Hegel's ambition to build a complete and comprehensive philosophical system, Kierkegaard remarked, "I've just got some corns – that at least is a step in the right direction..."

One reason why Kierkegaard is enjoying a resurgence is his quest for the meaning of life on its own terms. The crucial question is not what shall we live on, but what shall we live for? His interest is in "the individual". In itself society is nothing, comprising as it does a series of individual, independently employed, responsible people. They are not "examples" of the human race but the most concrete entities that exist, enabling Kierkegaard to claim that "Subjectivity is Truth". This does not mean of course that everything is relative and a thing is only true because one believes it to be so, but that noone can escape from reality without deceiving themselves. Each individual must make the crucial choice to take up their own life and understand themselves as guilty creatures – guilty both of what they do and of what they omit to do.

Concepts such as love, responsibility and guilt, in fact all moral concepts, only make sense in relation to people. A society as such cannot really be guilty of anything. But the individuals within that society – be they politicians, voters, law-

breakers or law-abiders – can be guilty of all manner of things, both of what they do and of what they omit to do. And in the deeper sense that is what they are. All are guilty, all have a responsibility. They are of course not guilty of all manner of things and do not have responsibility for everything, but all are guilty of something. "We hold part of our neighbour's life in our own hands," says the Danish philosopher, K.E.Løgstrup (1905-81).

The Danes as individualists

If we search the past for the cultural roots of modern Denmark we meet a conspicuous tradition for thinking of the individual as an independent creature, relatively irrespective of their actual social status. The individual has a weight and an importance, and human life has a precious quality to it – even in its highly incomplete representation in the concrete person. We are more than just figures on a board.

This cultural feature has also left its mark on the fundamental philosophy of education that has characterized upbringing and education in Denmark over the past two centuries. Like many other countries Denmark has an educational tradition of cathedral schools and grammar schools that goes back to the Middle Ages, but from the early 1800s there is an educational tradition that is distinguished by an almost anti-authoritarian self-awareness and peasant imperviousness to the Latin tradition. The Enlightenment idea of giving authority to the people receives a regional stamp containing a concession to Danish mentality. By the 1780s a number of visionary and unprejudiced educationalists are introducing experimental schools to practise the Enlightenment ideas. One of them was Count Ludvig Reventlow (1751-1801) who opened a school on his manor Brahetrolleborg in the 1780s with the aim of making the pupils not only good and useful citizens but also "happy people". To speak of "happiness" in this context is a fair way from Kant's demand that education should produce authority. Happiness is a concept that in its openness mitigates towards the individual's life potential. To focus on individual happiness involves rejecting education as an instrument, whatever the advantage to society of setting up popular schools.

Denmark acquired its democratic constitution in 1849.

In the pioneer Education Act of 1814 therefore, we hear the unmistakable tones of the absolute state seeking to make its pupils "good, honest citizens" and "useful citizens in the state". But in the course of the century it becomes clear that education is gradually making itself independent of that overriding state consideration. Historically, education develops alongside the growing freedom of the peasantry, set loose from their parish-tie in 1788, and allowed to move around the country. The independent peasant culture added to educational thought of the time an element of self-awareness.

A distinguishing mark of Danish education over the past 150 years has been that the Enlightenment emphasis on reason and encyclopaedic book knowledge did not stand alone but was seriously modified by a romantic understanding of the relationship between mankind and the world – an understanding that pointed more towards the mysterious, unfathomable life that we humans live out with one another. Denmark has a special tradition for understanding popular education as different from and more than a rational acquisition of factual knowledge. The central motif is "life enlightenment" – an interest in a deep understanding of life without resorting to patented truths. Science can teach us *how* life hangs together, and here we use our reason. But faced with the more fundamental question that reality exists, and that we exist within it, we must all capitulate – expert and layman alike.

The close Danish link between popular education and life enlightenment receives tremendous nourishment from N.F.S. Grundtvig above all, and from the immediate fruits of his educational thought which produced the Danish Folk High School, Denmark's most original contribution to education (see chapter 8).

Grundtvig
and the growth of education

Nikolaj Frederik Severin Grundtvig (1783-1872) is a central and highly significant character in Danish culture. In the course of a long life he was committed on many fronts: as a priest, a writer, a poet, a historian, a philologist, an educationalist and a politician. In contrast to his more famous contemporaries, Hans Christian Andersen and Søren Kierkegaard, he is relatively unknown outside Denmark. Yet his influence on Danish culture and thought can hardly be overestimated. In practice every area of our culture has been affected by his work, including our ideas about schools and education, our politics and our church life. It is difficult to say with certainty to what depth Grundtvig has changed our way of thinking and being, but our love of life, our cheerfulness, democratic thought, spiritual freedom and broad-mindedness would have had considerably less room for movement without the visionary power that emanated from his poetry, his songs, his hymns, books and speeches.

Some people are born old and paradoxically seem to become younger with age. The American writer Henry Miller said that it took him 45 years to become young; until then he had been prejudiced and pig-headed, unwilling to embrace life without a defence capability and a permanent mental reservation. To some extent this is also true of Grundtvig. Had he died at the age of 45 he would still be among the more interesting characters in Danish culture, but he would not have had the penetrating power as a cultural reformer that he has since been granted. By then he had published books on history, theology and mythology and had written a number of religious poems set to music as songs and hymns.

The crucial change came between 1829 and 1831 when in his late forties he made three trips to England to pursue his interest in Old Nordic literature. He spent a considerable time at Trinity College, Cambridge, studying various original manuscripts and enthusing over the spirit of learning that suffused the university. In particular he admired the close, almost confidential relations between teacher and student, marked as they were by mutual respect. A student's admiration for his teacher was natural, but a teacher's interest and respect for his student was new to Grundtvig. He thought that perhaps it had something to do with them both living on or near the same campus, allowing them to meet not just for the formal teaching but also in the less formal circumstances of the dining-hall, the park, afternoon tea, or even the playing-fields.

The spiritual climate at Cambridge differed fundamentally from Grundtvig's experience of Danish education at grammar school in Århus and university in Copenhagen. A few years after his visit to England he wrote to King Frederik VI proposing the establishment of a Danish academy on English lines for future civil servants. They would sit alongside the sons and daughters of the people and get to know their needs, thereby enabling them to administer the state in the interests of the people rather than against them. The idea was not taken up at the time, but was later developed into what became known as the *højskole*, the Folk High School of Denmark.

This plain and cheerful, active life on earth

Grundtvig's personal rejuvenation reached its spiritual zenith through a meeting with Clara Bolton at a dinner-party in London in 1830. A beautiful, thoughtful woman in her late twenties Clara was married to a successful doctor who later become private physician to the British prime minister, Disraeli. In the course of a deep conversation that to the surprise of the other guests lasted all evening Grundtvig and Mrs Bolton discussed life here and hereafter. They disagreed, to put it mildly. Grundtvig promoted his relatively traditional Christian view that our earthly life is only a temporary and limited enterprise compared with the life to come in paradise. Being an educated "modern" woman Mrs Bolton argued that such a view of Christianity turned its back on life; instead we should learn from the heroic figures of Greek and Nordic mythology, who live and act and dare to look their destiny in the eye without flinching. Grundtvig was enchanted by her looks, but equally by her argument. He melted down his previous views and rebuilt them in her image.

It sounds like a good story, but it happens to be true. And the encounter has been a kind of yeast for Danish culture in the intervening 150 years. Doubtless Grundtvig was already on the way to changing his views, but it appears to be this single meeting – and personal infatuation – that turned his head and pointed him in a different direction. For him life now became the crucial battlefield, and Christian faith the weapon that set free the individual to live that life to the full. Life: the word appears again and again in his speeches, articles, sermons, songs and hymns, and he claps his hands in unconditional joy, so to speak, at the gift of life as we experience it through our senses, our intellect and our spirit. There is nothing exalted about it, but Grundtvig has in mind a love of what the modern Danish poet Klaus Rifbjerg calls "this pallid, absinthe-coloured, lecherous, perverse, wonderful, brutal life".

This overwhelming joy in life is seen as the hallmark of Grundtvig's philosophy, spreading as it does to most areas of our existence, including upbringing and education, church life and politics. From now on he dedicates himself to whatever has to do with life, from everyday political matters to the nature of eternity.

One of Grundtvig's basic tenets is that reality is not something one tries to find out *about* but something one gets *into*. A rational approach to reality has its clear limits: one can find out about it, but what then? Much better to involve oneself in it, for which purpose love is required. It is love, says Grundtvig, that gives insight. What makes our life rich and significant are all the things that we are able to declare our love for. The more we care for in life, the greater its riches. Love creates an intimacy with this mysterious and unfathomable life that we have been granted. As he writes in one of his most famous poems:

> The glitter that the world now bows before
> by word and thought, by fate and deed ensnared,
> I would not wish for you, dear children, nor
> for anyone other soul for whom I cared...

> I would not for a king's existence trade
> this plain and cheerful, active life on earth,
> enlightened by the path our fathers' laid,
> in castle or in hut with equal worth.

Grundtvig wrote these lines for his children's confirmation in 1839 as a sort of speech in poetic form. Shortly before his death he was asked to turn parts of the poem into a song, which, beginning with the second quatrain quoted, proved to be one of his most popular. Over these powerful lines rests a certain pride and self-awareness, encouraging the singer to measure his or her life with a king's – or anyone else's for that matter. For each of us has a fundamental value and dignity, each of us has a life in which we are the main actor; we cannot live anyone else's.

But is not this to pretend that there is no difference between King Solomon and Tom, Dick or Harry? For clearly some are greater than others. To which Grundtvig would respond that each of us is a precious, divine experiment, the results of which are not known beforehand. No one has a patent on how to live or a set of instructions on how to assemble life. Life's meaning must flow from what we can work out together through a lifelong conversation about "this plain and cheerful, active life on earth".

The plainness of man is a common theme in Grundtvig, but plainness should in no way be construed as a synonym for mediocrity or lack of talent. It has more to do with qualities than qualifications. The Danish Nobel prizewinner for physics, Niels Bohr, was known to be a plain man, but he was no ordinary scientist. For him life was not a means to an end but the end itself. We do not live to work but work to live, and all human endeavour should serve this end; society, commerce, politics, science and education. Grundtvig's philosophy of life is down-to-earth, and as such it lies like a permanent seed-bed under Danish culture.

FINISHING TOUCHES

Global grook

If we want Peace,
the things we must
accomplish
to preserve it
are, first,
to win each other's trust
and, second,
to deserve it.

Piet Hein

2. The Foundations of Learning – 3 to 8

Agnete Engberg

A little child in Denmark is planned, wanted and usually loved. The child's parents are normally adult and established; they live together but are not necessarily married. Every other newborn child comes into the world out of wedlock, but as the child moves up through school age most of the parents are married.

Families in Denmark are small. In addition to one's parents there is usually a sister or a brother, and only these two generations live together. The older generation live separate from their children's family and have their own life of work and leisure, but they are normally very interested in the upbringing of the new child.

The family is a private area, where feelings may be shown and where there is a consciousness of an existential interdependence. Young parents are exempt from practical and financial responsibility for their elders, but great importance is attached to their responsibility and care for the coming generation.

Welcome to the child: the early years

It is regarded as a basic human condition to be a child in a family and later to reproduce; indeed it is seen almost as a right to have children, a basic condition for the quality of life.

In relation to previous generations more women now give birth to and raise at least one child. If this is not biologically possible the health service is expected to provide treatment for infertility, or the problem is solved by adopting a foreign child. Such efforts to acquire a child are as a rule expensive for both the couple and the public health service.

The child is thus the object of much attention and interest, not only from the mother (over 90% of Danish women give birth to a child before they are 40) but to a great degree from the father. Nowadays fathers see themselves much more as carers than in previous generations, where, as sole breadwinner in the family, they had limited contact with the small child.

In Danish tradition and consciousness the nuclear family is the corner-stone of society. But it is not as solid and lifelong a unit as in previous generations. In the past marriages ended with the death of a partner; in our time this happens when the couple part or get divorced. Because unmarried relationships (paperless marriages) are not registered, we lack precise knowledge of the number of dissolutions involving children. But the assumption is that roughly one-third of Danish children will experience a divorce or a dissolution before their 18th year. There are actually very few single mothers. Normally the child grows up in a home with both biological parents. Many of the children living apart from their mother or (more often) their father nevertheless grow up in a nuclear family with another adult in what may be termed a composite family. Adults' separation and establishment of new relationships takes place over a period of time, so while 90% of the 0 to 2-year-olds live with both biological parents, only around 70% of 15 to 17-year-olds do so.

There is still constant discussion as to what is best for children who don't see both parents on a daily basis. On the one

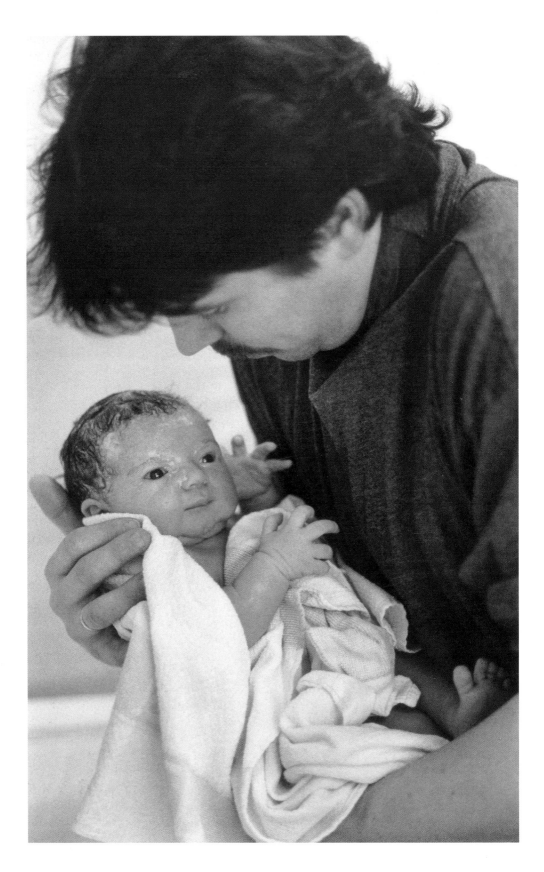

hand it is maintained that the child has a right to the care and interest of two parents, and parents need to follow their child's growth closely. On the other hand there is experience to prove that adults find it difficult to manage their emotions in such cases, and that joint-custody children can become disturbed and insecure.

The position of the child as being wanted and valuable takes many forms. There are many traditions linked to children and the various growth stages are noted: the first tooth, the first step, the first word. Children's birthdays bring the family together, and everything is registered and documented in photos, videofilms and notes.

The child's daily life is marked by a high degree of consumption: of clothes, hygienic items, baby and child food, toys etc. On the other hand many parents experience a lack of time when a new child arrives in the home. Everyday life can come under pressure for both parents and child, due usually to the parents' concern for their work. Practically all parents have a job, with young fathers working on average more than the rest of the population and 80% of mothers with children under 10 having a job, most of them full-time. Only a third work part-time, so that even in a period of high unemployment such as has recently been experienced mothers still see themselves as part of the labour market. They must be available to take a job at short notice and therefore require stable help with care and upbringing once the 6-month maternity leave is over.

There is thus a conflict of interests between the parent's wishes and their actual lives. A number of surveys have shown that parents would prefer to have more time together with their children and to spend less time at work every day. With the increased striving for job equality, part-time work is also the express wish of many young fathers. But such ideas are unworkable since there is no one to carry either the financial costs or the consequences for job equality. The closest we can get to realising the wish for more time with the children is through job-leave, which is proving popular with both men and women with children under the age of 8. Job-leave offers the legal right to withdraw from and then return to work. So far it is mainly women who have availed themselves of the opportunity, but the major employment organisations are also growing positive about the idea on the fathers' behalf.

Being together with one's children is thus acquiring greater significance throughout the population. To have influence over one's children also has a high priority in both legislation and practice, with parents participating in the management of both nurseries and schools.

Care and upbringing by parents and society

With the parents of small children being so economically active there is a general demand on society to provide an extensive and qualified educational system for the family. Thus from infancy it is normal for others to look after the child – from the day-care woman, publicly controlled and paid, looking after infants in her private home, to the institutions that care for 80% of all 2 to 3-year-olds during the day.

These creches and nurseries have their historical basis in the local groups, both public and private, that became so widespread that the state and local councils gradually took over their management and financing, although a third are still run by local or national organisations.

Characteristic of Danish society is the fact that in practically every area there are alternatives and new initiatives driven by the desire or sense of duty among people to do something for themselves and unselfishly to look after others who need their solidarity and support. The public sector will often respond with financial and professional backing. In this "third network", the area between the private sphere of families and the public sphere, there is a high degree of commitment and expertise. So the Danish child often meets adult society through volunteers who via their organisation or institution help to supplement the child's upbringing at home.

This development has now reached the point where "guaranteed places" are being promised politically. This is now a state demand on the local councils and it is only a matter of a few years before all children from the age of 2 will have a nursery place if their parents so desire.

The general agreement on sharing the child's upbringing raises questions of common goals and content as well as quality. Will parents and/or the state gradually demand the introduction of a nursery curriculum preparing children for the Folkeskole, the national comprehensive school from 6 to 16, or will there still be wide differences in the values and cultural influences that small children at present meet?

Unlike most other European countries Denmark has no fixed content, nationally determined, as to what day-care or nursery care should comprise. This raises many problems, but it does also allow for great freedom to bring quality to the children's daily life – and also not to.

Present-day parents are quality conscious and demand influence over their child's daily life. There is a running dialogue between parents and nursery teachers where the latter can give advice to unsure or inexperienced parents.

By tradition parents occupy a strong position in relation to nurseries and schools. There is legislation that confers on parent councils the authority to make decisions about finance and the educational content of nursery care. There is no real premise for assuming anything about a common

Danish culture for pre-school children. Previously there was a specialist course for training pre-school teachers, but this was abolished by parliament.

The Danish nursery tradition has built very much on the theory and practice of Fröbel, seeing the child as a growing individual whose abilities should be strengthened and developed. This sits well alongside Grundtvig's view of children and education; and indeed both developed around the same time at the end of the last century, though in different circles. Grundtvig's ideas were developed into the Folk High School out of a rural background, while the kindergarten movement grew in the cities as the daughters of the bourgeoisie began their fight for emancipation in the 1870s. Nurseries are regarded – indeed have often regarded themselves – as a more radical phenomenon in the social picture. From very early on the progressive wing of the labour movement took the concept to its heart, whereas the more conservative wing saw no reason to introduce nurseries as a weapon in the emancipation either of women or the children themselves.

This radical tradition is still alive to a degree: in the insistence on developing the child through an interaction in play and in the experience of meeting with the culture and nature of the country. However, this view of the nursery as a place of learning and development is to some extent offset by the political pressure to provide care pure and simple as the primary aim, with the emphasis laid on the parents' job situation and on flexible opening hours. In this context the question of evening and even night nurseries is being discussed, which makes it absurd to talk of cultural content and a common curriculum.

Into the Folkeskole

At the same time, however, the philosophy of the nursery has been welcomed into the Folkeskole in the form of a 1-

year, voluntary, nursery class which is now taken by practically all children from the age of 5 up to 7. Slower and faster children mix irrespective of their age and move from here into the 1st and 2nd class. After three years their maturity level is more or less the same, and they move on through the school with their classmates. The interest in this "coordinated school-start" is spreading.

The Folkeskole receives the new children as individuals from what may be widely varying backgrounds, with their skills and potential, their families, cultures and traditions. By law teachers must work with the individual pupil, formulating an individual tuition that enables the child to get the best out of the classroom work. But this demand is impossible to live up to, for simultaneously the teacher must ensure that the children learn to live in communities, and in an open, democratic and tolerant culture.

Children of 5 to 7 are of course not blank pages. They have already met many adults, teachers and their assistants and experienced various children's groups in often quite different organisations. With their knowledge, skills, attitudes and experiences they have learned how to express themselves and affect their surroundings, forming the basis for their 9-year school career.

There is always a lively debate in the country about the Folkeskole and the teacher's role. For all parents are pundits, with a personal experience from the past, a view on what the school down the road is doing to or for their child, and an awareness of the traditional values of Danish education over generations. The aims and values of education are a sort of social creed, with politicians and citizens debating their merits and defects while the children carry on unaware, depending on adults in their family, school and leisure to prepare them for their future.

In the early years there are only two worlds: the home and nursery school. Both these cultures are informal and close, with experiences being made outside any form of system. At school children begin to meet the subject division of the adult world, and their timetable becomes compartmentalised into Danish, Science, Arithmetic, Craft, Music and so on. Each subject has its syllabus, but teachers are required to work across the syllabus where possible, so several subjects meet in one particular theme. This needless to say is easier said than done.

Among the child's clear expectations of school is the mastering of technology. It becomes important to be able to read the sub-titles on TV and in the cinema (no foreign films are dubbed in Denmark, so foreign language attainment comes more naturally). Calculation becomes important for making a wooden boat or getting the right change from a sweets machine. The child has a large number of theories as to how the world hangs together and great curiosity for all kinds of phenomena.

But it cannot be denied that a compartmentalised day of 45-minute lessons in various subjects, each followed by a 10-minute break in an asphalt playground with ½ hour for lunch, is an artificial environment for school-starters, and possibly puts a brake on the development of some of them.

With the arrival of school comes another new concept: leisure. This is a new way of looking at the world, and a dimension that may present a problem for carers: who is responsible for the child, and what should the free time be used for?.

Since the introduction of the nursery class at school in 1966 society has found it hard to answer these questions. The nursery world and the school world could perhaps be better combined as regards developmental, cultural progress – the vertical context. Here we might well turn back to the experiences of the first nurseries at the beginning of the 19th century and make the nurseries more structured and the school more play-minded.

However, we have not yet managed to make the child's day hang together in time and content – the <u>horizontal context</u>. The spare time mentioned above is not in fact the child's to decide what to do with. It is even debatable whether in their early school years children need a life separate from caring adults. To wander around without "control" in the wild, adventure landscape is hardly a "need", and parents shudder as a rule at the thought of their 5 to 8-year-old children being free in that sense. For even though children by this age have acquired a certain independence and judgement, for example in traffic or their choice of friends, they are not yet ready on their own to take up the various cultural options and play without help from adults. Conflicts cannot be solved with a dignified result for those concerned without considerable experience and linguistic ability.

For most children the schoolday is relatively short, only 4 or 5 lessons. There are therefore various opportunities for a reasonably eventful afternoon for children: some schools organise leisure-time pursuits including music and sport. In other areas it is the social welfare council that performs the task. In addition comes the wealth of pursuits from many and various quarters, often with an ideological content. These include scouts and guides, sports clubs, swimming baths, dance, interest groups of various kinds and wide-ranging activities at local libraries, including story-telling and drama. From the age of 3 children are familiar with various forms of children's theatre and music schools, which are supported by the state and the local councils. As the cultural market opens up for children they learn from an early age to pick and choose, to test and absorb or discard. Their rooms are full of toys and magazines and technology of various kinds, often including computers.

The Danish children's programmes on TV have been a common cultural platform for many young children and their parents, creating a kind of norm by which other offers are measured. As they grow, their horizons widen and parents find it hard to control their consumption. Especially since they themselves are children of the multi-media generation.

Yet there is nothing to compare with the personal, direct contact of being together with an adult whom the child likes – reading aloud, playing together, working in the kitchen or the garden. This creates the solid foundation for the upbringing of the older child, who naturally turns to the wider world, to friends and companions, and who is allowed a wider radius of freedom.

20th century changes

There have been three major changes during the century with regard to children's lives, changes which adults have not always been able to cope with and which have often caused inner and outer conflicts.

The first change is in the family itself, even though it remains the basis for linking children and parents close together.

The second change is in the status of children. They are now individuals with rights promoted by the UN convention: to protection, to faith, to freedom of speech and assembly. Even the smallest child in a sense becomes a citizen – though without political influence and responsibility. There is a general acceptance now that we must listen to children, both in the family and in the community. There are local children's councils, and at school pupils' councils have a lengthy history. For children in need there are open advice bureaus and hot-line services. When the parents no longer live together, children have some influence on where they themselves shall live. Corporal punishment was abol-

ished in schools in the late 1950s, and in 1997 banned by law within the home too. The debate goes on, as it is clear that this change in children's legal status raises new questions as to the content of the parents' authority and the extent of the child's responsibility.

The third change is that the public sector, society, now shoulders co-responsibility for the child through practical, financial and moral channels. There is general agreement on this with regard to both legislation and finance, and politicians and social authorities are busy working out a specific children's policy, which is not always identical with family policy. Children's interests are not always best served through their parents.

The financial and practical provision of day-care and schooling is a corner-stone of society, but other areas also exist where resources are made available to parents and children. A maintenance allowance is paid to mothers and fathers on the birth of a child and there are a number of health programmes, child treatment, vaccinations and so on to ensure the child's healthy welfare.

The state pays a tax-free child allowance for all children up to the age of 18 whatever the parents' income. In 1997 this amounted to 10,500 DKK p.a for 0 to 3-year-olds, and somewhat less for older children. Economic support is also made available to single breadwinners, while there are many kinds of help available to handicapped children.

Large amounts are paid from both public and private money to support libraries, musical activities and so on, while both sport and TV are considered developmental assets for children.

All these various offers are taken up and used most intensively by the better-off, even though they were envisaged from the start as a help for the weaker socio-economic groups. But the coverage is so extensive that almost everywhere it is seen as a general and wide-ranging scheme that practically all children participate in from an early age.

3. The Folkeskole – 6 to 15

Kaj Frederiksen & Bent Brandt Jensen

The Folkeskole was founded in 1814, when all children were given the right to seven years of education in reading, writing, arithmetic and bible study. Since then only 5 major changes have been made, through Education Acts in 1903, 1937, 1958, 1975 and 1994.

The latest Act provides a 9-year basic education for all children in Denmark from 6 to 15, with an optional 10th year. As an introduction to their new school children can go to a nursery class for a year, an option taken up by over 95% of all parents. All schools are comprehensive, and all children progress automatically from one year to another whatever their attainment in a subject. They thus remain together for 9 years sharing experiences with one another and with the class teacher who follows them through the school.

Decentralisation

Danish society is characterised by a high degree of decentralisation. Legislation often takes the form of a framework, to be filled out by local administration. This goes for the Danish Folkeskole – a common, national school with a local stamp. The purpose of the framework legislation is to allow as many people as possible with a stake in the Folkeskole to take responsibility for the basic education of the coming generation.

Aims and frames

Parliament sets the national aims and frames that become the law for the nation's schools and the subjects they teach. Education Acts are by and large approved by both the government and the opposition in a broad political majority. Close cooperation between parents, teachers and pupils is required by law.

Curricula and teaching guidelines for the individual subjects are then worked out by expert committees including practising teachers and approved by the Ministry of Education, but how the aims are to be achieved – the methods and the means – is left to local administration.

The purpose of the Folkeskole is to give children the basic knowledge and skills to function in a democratic society. There is no compulsory schooling, only compulsory teaching – a democratic right which Danish parents occasionally assert by teaching their children at home. But of the 10% of children who do not attend the Folkeskole, the vast majority go to private schools. These, while being administered privately, offer the same curriculum as the Folkeskole, and receive considerable funding from the state. School fees are minimal; most parents can afford them if they so choose. There is no particular status attached to private schools, nor are their results significantly better than in the state schools. They may offer a smaller, more secure environment, but their chief importance is in providing an alternative to the Folkeskole.

There are 275 local councils in Denmark, each of which must set out its aims for its local schools on the basis of the national legislation and its own finances. A fishing community on the west coast will not share the same local goals of a multi-cultural Copenhagen suburb. But there is still a further step in the decentralisation process, for the means and methods are actually in the hands of the indi-

vidual schools. They it is who within the financial limits set by the local council, set their own aims and and methods. Their priorities vary, as do their teaching breadth, their pupil intake, their parental support and their leadership's vision. Through close cooperation among all four parties involved each school develops its own culture and traditions and works out its own curriculum and teaching guidelines within the national frame.

Each school has a board of governors, elected every 4 years, which at quarterly meetings sets out the principles for the day-to-day running and the educational policies of the school.

Autonomous teachers

Alone or together teachers teach in accordance with the agreed aims. In such a decentralised system teachers are duty-bound only to the general aims of the Folkeskole and the individual subjects. They are therefore relatively independent and autonomous, which accounts for the high sense of commitment and responsibility that they feel. They are seen as professionals who have the right and duty to plan the content and methods of their teaching.

For decades now teachers' self-awareness has been based upon this freedom of choice, without outside interference. Over the years the number of examinations and grades given to pupils has gradually decreased, the trend being towards a minimal number of final examinations and grades. A possible replacement under consideration is an integrated assessment that does away with labelling pupils on the strength of a level achieved at a particular moment.

As long as there is general agreement in a school on its aims, values, content and methods, autonomy is an obvious advantage for teachers. In a society undergoing rapid change, however, there is no longer quite the consensus that there was, and

autonomy can be a liability insofar as the buck stops with the individual teacher.

Of course Danish teachers are not looking for a return to exact, measurable knowledge or precise, conservative methods, but it is crucial that the teachers' autonomy is supplemented by a large degree of responsibility from the other school bodies involved, not least the political and financial decision-makers. Otherwise the aims and methods will remain unclear, satisfaction with the school will fluctuate and the basic education of children be neglected.

New Folkeskole Act

In 1994 a new Education Act was passed for the Folkeskole which, following long-established tradition, came into being only after widespread canvassing of grass roots, including teachers. Proven experience formed the basis of the law, which aims to prepare children for an unpredictable future characterised by a technology explosion. Whatever the future requires in the way of knowledge and skills, youngsters must still live life for themselves and their community. So their personal, all-round development is central in the new act. Teaching must take the individual as its starting-point, and must also ensure that all children find their place in the community.

Cooperation

The keyword therefore is cooperation among all the adults around the child, and between the child and the adults. This is the reason for talking of a new teacher role. Teaching is still marked by autonomy, but the teacher's independence is no longer limitless. The demand now is that teachers plan their teaching together, both short-term and long-term, with a view to providing differentiated teaching (mixed ability teaching) for children on the basis of their level of development, needs and interest. In theory this gives each child an education not only in curriculum subjects but also for personal and social development.

Goals must be specified for all children at every level. Teaching teams must cooperate with each other and the individual pupil and must evaluate the course and teaching as they go along. Pupils have a legal right to participatory democracy as well as a co-responsibility for their own learning.

The law requires that teaching should also be practical and creative and include the use of computers across the curriculum.

The leadership team is in charge of the educational content at the school and must ensure that all the teachers of a given class work together. The leadership must support and cooperate with the teachers, among other things through conversations and keeping abreast of the actual classroom teaching.

Change in work patterns

Since teaching in the Folkeskole must now be based on projects and cross-curricular cooperation, with teachers using their subject knowledge as only one element among others, it follows that the teacher is changing from being the omniscient cultural mediator to being the one who arranges, carries out and decides. Teachers now give the pupils space and opportunity to learn, in the belief that it is the doer who learns, while they themselves lead the teaching processes, but step back to allow the pupil to seek and act, to gain experience and learn from it. To be the actor of an action is a self-increasing process that develops skills old and new.

This teacher transition from sole authority for a subject-based learning to collaborating "process consultant" means that the teacher's command of didactics becomes even more important. Teaching must be carried out on the basis of a sys-

tematic theory and an ethical code; teachers must be able to defend their choices educationally through theoretical insight, knowledge and experience. To be aware of one's reasons is the prerequisite for defining one's teaching aims and methods.

Thus professional teachers must be able to: interpret and discuss the implementation of the curriculum at their school; enter into a committed collaboration with other staff; reflect on their own teaching experiences; and present those experiences openly for debate with their colleagues. Teachers must also be able to assess and evaluate what the pupils have learned and be able to document it.

Change in the concept of teaching

The concept of teaching itself is thus undergoing change, and with it the role of the teacher. Such a process is not easy for the individual teachers, who are used to regarding themselves as teachers in particular subjects. The new teacher role requires them to create transformations both in their own subjects and in their teaching psychology.

The reason for this change is, among other things, the new qualifications that youngsters need when they leave school: flexibility, readiness to change, ability to cooperate, linguistic and social competence, cultural insight and understanding – and of course skills in the cultural techniques of reading, writing and arithmetic, plus new technology.

Living up to these demands is important for every citizen in Denmark, as part of life in a modern, democratic society. But it is equally important to be able to live as a citizen in an increasingly open world community, where events in one place increasingly influence living conditions in another.

Another change is the increasing need for teachers to function as deputy parents. With most Danes out at work during the

day there is a huge demand for pre-school and especially after-school care, as some children are spending up to 12 hours a day away from home. At the other end of the spectrum are children of unemployed parents, growing up in homes where to be "out at work" is unknown and where the only income is unemployment benefit.

New thinking also characterises teaching approaches to the growing immigrant and refugee population, mainly from the Middle East, whose parents need time to get to know the Danish language and culture. If and when they do so, they are not necessarily interested in their children becoming "Danish", with all that that implies of freedom, democracy and responsibility.

The Future

With the average age of teachers now approaching 50 there is a deep-felt need for major investment in technology and in-service training to meet these new demands, an educational and financial task which is in the hands of the local authorities. There will doubtless be a long series of compromises as dream meets reality. One of the strengths of the Danish system as the Danes see it has been the opportunity for a class to retain the same teacher in most subjects right through their school life. This has been made possible by the teacher's 4-year training to teach all classes at all levels in most subjects. So the teacher who welcomes a class of 6-year-olds may also be the one who waves goodbye to them aged 15. However, with the new Education Act urging greater specialisation this practice is under pressure and cannot survive for much longer.

Children's Diaries: Wednesday 5th April 1995

- Sidsel

Here I am. My name is Sidsel (pronounced Sissel, ed.). I'm 7, I go to school at Møllevangen. I've got three class teachers, one is Joan, the other is Lis and my music teacher is Ole. It's fun to go to school because I like my teachers. In Danish we're doing the letter capital H; then there are three words with h, like Hanne and hat and house.

We have arithmetic, we've done one arithmetic book, and the next one is a bit difficult. But my teacher helps me as best she can.

Then I have music. We sing the song about Kasper and Jesper and Jonathan, and the Bicycle Song about 10 little cyclists.

I want to tell you what I did in school today. When we got to the classroom we had to sit in our places. Thomas in our class had been on holiday. Lis (Lease, ed.) thought that he ought to tell us a bit about it. Then it was break-time. We played zombie. It's like tag, you just say zombie-tag, it's best to be a lot, otherwise it's no fun. It's most fun if we play under a sheet on a mattress. The boys are hardly ever caught, it's mostly the girls who get caught. The boys weren't interested any more, they played their own zombie. They played till the bell went, but the teacher didn't come so we played on. Hellen said all the time that someone had done a fart. She asked Maidah, she said "yes" and grinned. Then I got fed up playing zombie. Instead I went and looked in my old arithmetic book. Then at last the teacher came. She said that we should find at least three rules at school that we ought to keep. I think she was going to give them to someone in the office. But suddenly she got a pain in her tummy. She went into the corridor to talk to a teacher. We were sitting alone, but someone went out and told her that we couldn't keep quiet. She came in a moment later and said, "Have you found three rules?" Ann Sofie found most rules. I think they were good rules. I think nearly everyone said a rule. I can't remember my rule. But I remember a rule that we mustn't go outside the school area, that's what Tinh and Anajan did. Oh, I just remembered another rule. We mustn't play ball in the classroom. Then it was break again. We played inside. We played a bit wild, so a teacher came and told us to go out. But it wasn't me, it was Karina and Hellen and Maidah. When break was over and the teacher hadn't come, one of the boys, Kent, came and boasted how many goals he'd scored. It was my Danish teacher again. This time we had the workbook, we had to look up under h. I wasn't finished before it was lunchtime. Then we had lunch. I had pita with sausage and two carrots inside and an apple...

When the bell went (for end of school, ed.) I went to the children's centre. Lone asked if I would like to go to the Children's House. We got home (the children's centre, ed.) at 1.30. I rushed over to the climbing-frame, I was the fastest to get there and slide down. After a time some of the others from the centre came and we played. We played tag, but not for long. Then we began climbing. But in the end they couldn't be bothered any more. We took our socks off and climbed up the slide, we fell off a lot because there were some twists and turns. Then we went home to the children's centre. We went up to the homework room. We did my homework until my mum came and fetched me. When my mum had fetched me, it was time to go home and have dinner, because we were quite hungry. My mum thought that I hadn't eaten my bun that we bought yesterday. I bought a Polly Pocket (mini doll´s house, ed.) in Kvickly. I sat and played with it.

My mum's got a car. It's a Ford Fiesta. My mum's spent a lot of money on it, she's spent it on the back wheels and the brakes. My dad's also got a car, an Opel Corsa. It's red just like my mum's. My dad doesn't spend as much money on the car as my mum. I think he's got a lot of rust. Anyway he's got a lot of rust on the back. There's a very big hole. My dad's got a girlfriend, she's called Trine (Treena, ed.), she's got a girl who's 3 years old, she's called Sidsel like me and she's a Libra and a Virgin like me. One of my aunts is called Lone (Lowna, ed.), she's got a girl called Amalie who's a year old. I've also got a cousin. His mum's called Mona and his dad is Kim. His dad is my uncle. I was up at hospital to see when my cousin, she was very little. I wasn't pushed out that time. My cousin wasn't lying next to his mum, my cousin was in an incubator instead. I managed to see him, but then a nurse came and said it was best if I went. So I went out with Jens (Yens, ed.). That's my grandma, Anna-Lise's, boyfriend. We went out and bought some sweets. Then we drove in Kim's car. Then we stopped and had a burger. Then my mum and I drove home and Kim drove home.

Sidsel, aged 7
Århus.

– Vinh

My clock-radio started off by sending my favourite channel, P3 at 06.20, and after Rasmus Radiomouse I got up around 7 as usual. My Dad, he's a doctor at "the Kingdom" (University Hospital, ed.), was already up looking at some slides. Dad and I live alone in a "villa-flat". My Mum died when I was 7 and my big brother and sister, who are 28 and 29 respectively, both live in a big house in Herlev. All three of them came to Denmark from Vietnam at the beginning of the 70's so I'm half-Vietnamese.

I went out to the bathroom, had my usual shower, and 5-10 minutes later I pulled on a few clothes. I was pretty tired because I'd been writing a Danish essay late into the night.

Dad asked me what I wanted for breakfast. "Just egg and bacon", I said, half-asleep. For us egg and bacon means scrambled egg and bacon on toast. After breakfast Dad asked me to empty the washing-machine but I didn't have time as I had to do some German homework I hadn't done Tuesday night.

I managed to get off and was due at school at 08.10 for German. When I arrived at 08.08 there were only 3 or 4 others there (we weren't supposed to be many more because we divide up for German). Anyway, everyone managed to show up before the teacher arrived.

She asked us if we wanted to go to morning assembly (it's compulsory for nursery class to 7th, but I'm in 8th). We voted unanimously to go since that way we'd miss 10 minutes of the next lesson. At assembly we sang two songs from *555 Songs* – Today it's Sunshine and Rasmus the Duck, which the younger classes like.

After assembly it was time for Danish. We had read (or should have read) a story called "A Busy Ant". It was about an ant that followed its basic instincts. Our class teacher, who we also have for Danish and History, took the opportunity to tell us that on January 5th 1996 there would be a baby boom in Copenhagen. "Why?" we asked, and he said that it was because last night there had been a 4-hour power-cut in the city. He then gave us a whole load about how humans behave when they're left to themselves – all about Freud's three faces and the id and stuff like that.

After the next break it was Maths on the menu – some relatively easy problems and since we had a fair while to do them in, I managed to put the last two lines under the final solution as the bell went for the lunch break.

When you get to 8th class at our school, you're allowed outside during the lunch break from 10.45 to 11.20. I didn't buy anything, but there were plenty of others who did.

The next two lessons were Biology and Physics. The Ministry of Education has just made a rule that in 2 years time all classes will be doing a sort of project. Even though I won't be in 9th class in 2 years time our class at Lyngby Private School are doing one anyway. On the basis of this project assignment our class have had a short course on slide shows from our class teacher and our Biology teacher, and we worked on our slides during the Biology lesson.

In the Physics lesson we did Physics.

When I got home I finished my Maths and then I began to write my Wednesday diary. I nearly finished the first page but then I went off to tennis training at Lyngby Tennis Club.

When I came home again, I carried on with the diary, then had dinner with my Dad and then went off to Scouts (a pretty busy day!). I've been a scout for 8 years. We had a patrol meeting and although it was raining outside we did a relay with two of our three patrols choosing three people who had to go on 3-4 m long planks (skis) and reach the end before the other team. It was quite good fun (and

wet). Afterwards we just had sat around indoors: some of the others had made pancakes and buns, plus a good soup that really warmed up those who had got wet.

When I got home I finished writing my diary and now I'm going to fall s45678rtyuuidhfhgjkcnvmbb"(")(&) Oh my head...

Vinh, aged 14
Lyngby, Copenhagen

A Teacher's Diary: Thursday January 30, 1997

- Mogens Ballund

Strange that however much I love being a teacher I still want to stay in bed when the alarm goes at 6.30; and it's not much better when I get up at 6.40.

But after a shower and the first cup of coffee my thoughts tend towards the constructive. They have to. I've got five 45-minute lessons ahead of me and any sign of teacher tiredness is "punished" by the class getting restless, especially on a day like today where I start off with 2c for a double lesson. Maths and Science are on the timetable, but we don't take that too much to heart. It's nice to have two lessons in a row; we can really get some work done. Furthermore we have an assistant teacher – 2c's class teacher, who also teaches them Danish. Tina and I have 6 double lessons a week together, which is the main reason why the two of us not only have an excellent working relationship but why the class are getting more out of the subject and have realised that we are all functioning as a single unit.

Actually, it's also rather odd that although I hadn't taught "littluns" since 1972 – and had no desire whatsoever to do so – I now find I've been really happy with 2c ever since they arrived 1½ years

ago. I'd heard a lot about the children's new identity, their unreadiness for school and their lack of concentration. But at the risk of being accused of loss of memory I would maintain that the 21 children in 2c are not much different from the class I had a quarter of a century ago.

They're eager for knowledge, active, sweet, funny and attentive. They work well together, are looking for contact and are eminently teachable. Surprisingly, there's no problem for them sitting still and listening, so long as it's not for *too* long. And they're also good at independent work, bearing in mind that they're only 7 or 8 years old.

Of course on occasion they're noisy, restless and inattentive, but then who isn't? It's not typical of them to be so; they're actually rather good at respecting the limits around them.

At 8 o'clock Tina and I walk into the classroom to find that two of the children are away with flu. And the 19 that are left will also be reduced to 17 off and on in the course of the day because (yes, I'd forgotten) the school dentist has arrived for the twice-yearly check-up, so when the first two pupils are finished the next two go off.

Anyway, in we go and the first thing we hear is "Tina, Tina..." and "Mogens, Mogens..." Oh yes, there's always a lot they want to tell us, but we soon sort the wheat from the chaff. It may sound like we're not interested, but honestly, it's absolutely necessary, otherwise we'd never get started. Their desire and ability to talk – to tell – is so developed that they could carry on for hours unless we put a fairly swift stop to it. On other occasions we actually plan "talking lessons" so they get the chance to develop their skills.

Today we're going to measure the temperature of water in different containers. Yesterday each of the 7 groups in the class put 1 dl of water in a freezer, a refrigerator, a window-sill by the radiator, and in buckets in the corridor, in the class stockroom and outside on the lawn. Now each group measures the 6 different temperatures, puts the results down on a form, and we talk about what they have found out. For the last 20 minutes we do multiplication sums in our Maths book.

In the morning break Tina supervises the first 10 minutes indoors (for fruit consumption) and another teacher supervises the next 10 minutes outdoors for rushing around and shouting. I'm off to a meeting with the head about the approaching school party (I'm the chair of the school party committee). This is about the only time available for a meeting in a very busy day.

In the 5th class, where I'm the class teacher as well as the Danish and English teacher, we're working on poetry at the moment, writing poems about winter. The next two lessons will go with the Danish project (the timetable says Danish-English but we change it around to suit ourselves). Unfortunately we can't get into the computer room until the second of the two lessons because it's occupied by another class. We've got 12 computers, which is a bit frustrating when you've got 22 pupils – actually we're not 22 today, because two of them have been given a dispensation to go on a skiing trip with their parents to Norway and Austria respectively. There's no computer in our classroom and in all there are only 25 computers in the school for 490 pupils. Rumour has it that the Local Education Authority will be giving us an extra computer allocation next year – we live in hope! At the moment practice does not live up to the declared aim of the Minsitry of Education to integrate computer science into the day-to-day work of the classroom. Still, 5b are working well on the assignment and when the double lesson is over we agree that the project can be completed in one more lesson (when the two skiers have returned!).

Time for a ½-hour lunch break, or rather 17 minutes for me – 5b are in a particularly talkative mood today. It's not always easy just to leave them, and as their class teacher I'm of course interested to hear what's on their minds here and now. Actually, the staffroom is in a wing that's a fair distance away from the classrooms and the children, and what happens to them in the breaks is the responsibility of the playground supervisors. I was on duty yesterday, so today I can sit down at "my" table, have my packed lunch and chat to a younger colleagues about this and that – but not the children or the teaching. No, we relax in peaceful surroundings. Whether or not it's a good idea to have the staffroom relatively distant from the children is debatable, but they rarely interrupt us, so it's a good place to recuperate.

In the fifth lesson I have Maths with 8th class. The 19 pupils sit at group tables working on equations, which we went through last lesson. For the first time today I must admit I have a lesson where I actually earn my money fairly easily. The pupils are working well and those who may have problems get just as much help from their classmates as from me, as I wander round the class.

After the lesson I've arranged a planning session with Tina for 2c, including a cross-curricular project for the spring and a parents' meeting for February 19th. Since Tina and I get on well, we're finished after 1½ hours; it's a bonus that teaching is no longer just a one-man job but involves a whole team dealing with each class.

I've just got to copy some material for 5th class tomorrow before I leave the school at 3.15 pm. It's been a good day, but I know how I'll be feeling at 6.30 tomorrow morning.

The Aims of the Folkeskole, 1994 Act

1.(1) The Folkeskole shall – in cooperation with the parents – further the pupils' acquisition of knowledge, skills, working methods and ways of expressing themselves and thus contribute to the all-round personal development of the individual pupil.

(2) The Folkeskole shall endeavour to create such opportunities for experience, industry and absorption that the pupils develop awareness, imagination and an urge to learn, so that they acquire confidence in their own possibilities and a background for forming independent judgments and for taking personal action.

(3) The Folkeskole shall familiarize the pupils with Danish culture and contribute to their understanding of other cultures and of man's interaction with nature. The school shall prepare the pupils for active participation, joint responsibility, rights and duties in a society based on freedom and democracy. The teaching of the school and its daily life must therefore build on intellectual freedom, equality and democracy.

2.(1) The Folkeskole is a municipal responsibility. The municipal authorities are responsible for ensuring all children in the municipal area receive free education. The municipal councils decide on the aims and targets of the schools' activity within this Act.

(2) The individual school is responsible for the quality of the teaching within the given framework, and plans the organization of the education.

(3) Parents and pupils cooperate with the school to fulfil the aims of the Folkeskole.

Compulsory Subjects

The teaching in the nine-year basic school shall cover the following subjects for all pupils.

1. a) Danish at all class levels
   b) English at the 4th to 9th class levels
   c) Christian Studies at all class levels
   d) Social Studies at the 9th class level

2. a) PE and Sport at all class levels
   b) Music at the 1st to 6th class levels
   c) Art at the 1st to 5th class levels
   d) Textile Design, Wood/Metal work and Home Economics at one or more class levels within the 4th to 7th class levels

3. a) Mathematics at all class levels
   b) Science at the 1st to 6th class levels
   c) Geography and Biology at the 7th and 8th class levels
   d) Physics/Chemistry at the 7th to 9th class levels
   These pupils shall be offered German at the 7th to 9th class levels
   The pupils may be offered instruction in French instead of German at the 7th to 9th class levels

The weekly number of periods for the pupils is at least:
1) 20 periods in pre-school and 1st and 2nd years.
2) 22 periods in the 3rd year.
3) 24 periods in the 4th and 5th years.
4) 26 periods in the 6th and 7th years.
5) 28 periods in the 8th, 9th and 10th years.

The school principal has to ensure that the class teacher and other teachers together plan and organize the teaching so that it has challenges for all pupils.

At every level and in every subject the teacher and the pupils cooperate to set the targets to be achieved. Methods of work and subject matter are agreed upon by teacher and pupils together.

The class teacher is given one period per week to take care of special problems and to attend to special needs and interests of the class.

School books and other educational material is made available to the pupils free of charge.

Every school has a school board consisting of 5-7 parents, 2 elected teachers and 2 pupils.

Teacher Training Act 1997

The course lasts 4 years and covers the following subjects:

Christian Studies

Either Danish or Maths

3 other subjects

1 dissertation in conjunction with one of the 4 subjects with pedagogical aspects

General Didactics, Psychology, Methodology and School in Society

Teaching Practice

The students must be given the option of a course in Music, Writing and Rhetoric as well as Adult Teaching.

The new idea behind the latest Teacher Training Act is to strengthen teachers' knowledge and skills in their respective subjects, so that they can take up the challenge of the 21st century and fulfil its demands for specialization as well as educate children for citizenship and national and global understanding within the culture of democracy.

4. A Cross-cultural Perspective on the Developmental Pressures of Danish Schooling

Steven Borish

In 1995-96 I completed a study of Danish social movements past and present, *Danish Social Movements in a Time of Global Destabilization*, building on my earlier work with the Danish Folk High Schools, *The Land of The Living: The Danish Folk High Schools and Denmark's Nonviolent Path to Modernization*. The educational component of my research focused on a special kind of Danish school called the Continuation School (the *efterskole*, literally, the "after" school). Two critical observations suggest the usefulness of using the Continuation School as the point of departure for a comparative perspective 1) It is a type of school found only in Denmark; and 2) it is a school form that has experienced an explosive growth in popularity in recent decades. In 1970 there were 6,000 students attending a Continuation School; in 1996 there were close to 20,000. In 1947 there were 68 such schools, in 1996 around 230. What kind of a school is this? Why are the schools found only in Denmark? What factors in Denmark lie behind their recent explosive growth in popularity? To what extent are these factors unique; to what extent do they represent a Danish development reflecting higher level international or global developments?

The Continuation School and the Folkeskole

A Continuation School is a boarding school, where young students from 14-18 years old can come for a year or perhaps two (this depends on the school), live collectively, and choose a course of study that can prepare them for the secondary level education that normally follows. In order to understand the particular nature of the Continuation School environment, it is important to be clear right from the very beginning about one of its distinguishing features: the dimension of personal choice. Attendance at a state-run public Folkeskole or a similar but independent private free school from 6 to 16 is the norm in Denmark. The stay at a Continuation School on the other hand is neither an automatic nor a routine consequence of simply being born in Denmark. The decision to go to such a school reflects a process which in terms of the Danish educational culture means that one has (together with one's parents) chosen an alternative to the normal course of events. What then is "the normal course of events" in Denmark? This question itself is worth a moment's reflection because it enables us to bring into sharp perspective some ways in which Danish education differs significantly from its United States' counterpart. The normal course of events in Denmark would be simply to continue on, taking the 9th and/or 10th class at either the public school or the particular kind of alternative free or private school one has been attending up to that point.

The Danish system and the American way

Some cross-cultural comparison will be helpful. In the United States the young person from 7th to 10th class is normally not required to make any major decisions about the type of school to be attended the following year. True, one chooses among different course options, and perhaps

even among different lines of study, but the normal American pattern is an automatic continuation from one school to another upon graduation. In the US one typically attends elementary school (1-5th class), middle school (6-8th class) and then high school (9-12th class). When finishing middle school at the end of 8th class, it is not necessary to make any application in order to be accepted at the local public high school. All who live within the residential boundaries of the local school district have the right to begin 9th class at the local public high school; they cannot be denied entrance.

The Danish system is very different. It gives students the option of completing the Folkeskole in either the 9th or 10th class. Frequently (although not always) the more academically inclined leave after 9th class, but it is possible to stay an additional year. So far, so good. But what really distinguishes Denmark from the United States is the requirement placed on Danish students that when they finish their 9 or 10 years of primary education (normally at the age of 15 or 16), they must already make major life decisions concerning their future.

If the Danish students wish to continue with their schooling – and the general expectation of both parents and society is that they will do so – it does not follow of itself that graduation from the Folkeskole gives them a place in the next higher school level. They themselves must first make a choice among alternatives, deciding whether they wish to attend an academic high school (Gymnasium), or a vocational school in the technical area (Technical School), or in the business area (Commercial School). This system not only requires that early life decisions be made in important areas, but that these decisions be actively followed up by passing one of the two Folkeskole leaving examinations; and in addition to preparing for them, the student must decide which

of them to sit and when. The primary school-leaving examination (Folkeskolens Afgangsprøve) is normally taken by those who leave after the 9th class. The extended primary school leaving examination (Folkeskolens Udvidet Afgangsprøve) is normally taken by those who leave after the 10th class.

This requirement for a relatively early decision forces young students to make important and often difficult choices that will have major implications for their future education and for their adult lives, as well as for their present conceptions of self – or their "ego identity" as Erving Goffman and E.H. Erikson call it in *Stigma* (1965). The transition to a higher level requires them to fill out applications for entrance into the next phase of schooling. The possibility of rejection on grounds of ability is always present, though not on grounds of limited availability. All pupils who are declared by the Folkeskole as being suitable for the next phase must be given places. At the same time the choice at 15 or 16 also commits students to a view of themselves and to a particular set of hopes, dreams and goals that are relevant both for the immediate and the long-term future.

All of these patterns are part of the particular cultural stress of adolescent development in Danish society. They manifest as intense stressors during early and mid-adolescence, typically at an age several years younger than students in the United States have to face their parallel stresses with university admission. In reality college-bound American students of this age, particularly those who are aiming for acceptance in an elite college, are already experiencing a high degree of stress for a different set of reasons - but unlike the Danish students, they do not have to make major career-oriented decisions concerning their immediate educational future. And although the actual choices are made when Danish students are 15 or 16, the cybernetic process that Eric Berne has called "reachback" implies that these stresses are very much in the minds of Danish 13 and 14-year-olds as well. In *What Do You Say After You Say Hello?* (1972) Berne has defined reachback as "that period of time during which an impending event comes to have an independent influence on the individual's behavior." In an earlier study of kibbutz adolescents, I saw another example of Berne's reachback: for many, and particularly the boys, the experience of formal education in the last two years of secondary school was deeply affected by the expected stresses of the required army service (3-4 years) that would follow graduation.

The Nordic model

The heightened stress of the decision-making process in early and mid-adolescence in Denmark may be unwittingly further intensified by another fundamental feature of Danish primary education: the fact that Danish children in the earlier years are in general given a higher level of care, support and attention than their American counterparts. In all Scandinavian countries the value of *omsorg* (care, nurturance, support), particularly in the years after 1960, has influenced educational goals, methods and practices. It is beyond the scope of this discussion to give a more detailed analysis of what Telhaug and Tønnessen in 1992 called "the Nordic model of education," but some of its major features include the following: 1) the focus on a child-centred education, with the child's autonomy and personal development viewed as being at the center; 2) the attempt to provide a home-like, warm and personal environment in the school and the classroom; 3) the emphasis on student democracy; 4) the conscious use of the school as an instrument for achieving social justice, including the areas of social and gender equality.

In support of these assertions about a cultural focus on a higher level of care and support as a primary goal of the Nordic educational model, one can point to three general Danish patterns which powerfully affect the school environment during early primary education. The first is the class teacher system, whereby a class of Danish children remains as a unit under the primary care of a single teacher from 1st class often until the 7th or 8th class (sometimes even longer). The teacher moves on with the class, beginning a new cycle again with younger children when the older children graduate. There is thus no such thing as a "teacher of 2nd years" in Danish educational culture. All teachers teach many classes, moving with their children. Few Danes, or other Scandinavians, would want to exchange this for the American pattern of a different teacher every year. When I told a Norwegian 4th class about the American system, one boy spoke forcefully for the class, saying, "We wouldn't be able to tolerate that!".

A second differentiating pattern of the Nordic school model is that in Denmark a child entering 1st class normally stays with the same class of children through all the succeeding years of Folkeskole school experience. Moreover, these pupils take all their classes in a single room, which comes to be seen both by them and by others as belonging to them, as their "homeroom" in the school. It is quite different in schools in the United States, where the teachers usually remain in, and are identified with, a single classroom, and the students move continually during the school day. The expressed goal of the Danish pattern is to give children a greater sense of security and stability in the early primary school experience, in particular a sense of belonging to a specific place in the school, and being able to assert certain territorial expectations concerning that place. I first became aware of this pattern on a visit to a Norwegian second-

ary school. Entering the room together with the teacher before the class, I chose a seat way in the back assuming it would belong to no one in particular. When the class entered, a very determined young lady marched up to me, informed me that I was sitting in her seat, and ordered me in no uncertain terms to vacate it at once. This behavior can be understood more clearly as a consequence of the home-room system, where not only the classroom but the seats become highly personalized forms of personal and group territoriality.

A third feature of the Nordic school model seen in Denmark is an attempt to downplay the impact of competition and inequality among students by postponing the giving of formal letter or grading evaluations until the 8th class. Until then, pupils receive informal evaluation in the form of written notes from the teacher with general comments, and conversations between the teacher, parents and pupil, but do not receive a letter or number grade.

Can these comparative observations about the relationship between stress, schooling and the life cycle be fitted into a framework which provides insight into the recent popularity of the Continuation School? One theoretical language that enables us to fit these and other previous observations together has been provided by the American anthropologist, George Spindler. In *Adolescents: Readings in Behavior and Development* (1970) Spindler has distinguished between what he calls periods of "compression" and "decompression" in the life cycle. Compression phases are marked by increased cultural stress, often accompanied by tightened role expectations, a narrowing of previously permitted behaviors, and the taking on of new responsibilities and obligations. Severe puberty initiation rites and military boot camps provide clear examples of what is meant by "cultural compression". Phases of cultural decompression on the other hand are accompanied by a relative relaxation of stress: individuals are given the time to unwind from an earlier compression state and to be sociable without the special pressures of the compression frame.

Identity pressure

Using Spindler's language of compression and decompression, I offer the following speculative hypothesis. Danish children in general experience greater cultural decompression in the early years of schooling than their American counterparts. They are not tested as much, are afforded greater continuity in social relationships with others, may call teachers by their first names instead of formal titles, etc. On the other hand, Danish young people between the ages of 13 and 16 generally experience greater cultural compression than their American counterparts. My hypothesis is that the contrast between the tendency for marked cultural decompression in the early years of schooling in Denmark, followed by the tendency for marked cultural compression in the years of mid-adolescence, creates a special kind of perception of discontinuty which comes to constitute an intense identity pressure on Danish adolescents. It is this type of developmental situation with its subtle discontinuities - as perceived by adolescents themselves - which in part has paved the way for the new and extremely active role played by the Continuation School. It is estimated that nearly 25% of a year intake of 9th and 10th class in Denmark are now taking that year at a Continuation School. One must always be extremely careful about making these kinds of cultural comparisons, but as an anthropologist with considerable experience both in American and Scandinavian schools, I believe this generalization holds. It may be helpful in explaining the particular nature of the transitions required by Danish young people as they move through their own educational system. Much of the intense popularity of the Continuation School must be understood in relation to this earlier need for the making of important life decisions on the part of young students.

An additional relevant factor is that the Danish system has evolved to contain a higher degree of post-primary school flexibility, manifested in a much greater range of possible choices available to students in the 9th and 10th class trying to decide on their futures. In addition to the three possibilities mentioned above, they can go out and work for a few years and then take a special 2-year alternative to the academic Gymnasium; this Higher Preparatory course (HF) is characterized by greater flexibility and an older, more experienced student group. They can go right away to one of the special Folk High Schools, or in a few years to one of the new Folk Day High Schools. They can attend a Production School, a special type of school that teaches industrial craftwork, or they can simply leave the country and try to see the world, perhaps seeking work abroad, perhaps travelling, perhaps doing both. As if all these were not enough, a recently designed and governmentally supported alternative (Free Youth Training FUU) allows those under 25 to design their own completely individualized course of education, combining, for example, 6 months at a Folk High School with 3 months of work abroad at a factory and then back to Denmark again for a year of schooling in industrial chemistry. Paradoxically, this remarkable freedom, great flexibility and wide range of choice can also lead to greater stress and uncertainty on the part of the young students of 13 and 14, who are faced with having to decide between all these possibilities.

In summary: the Continuation School represents a way of temporarily leaving behind the home, the school and the local neighborhood environment directly connected with the pressure of these decisions, which in many cases young people do not feel that they are ready to make. It enables them to come into a new and challenging situation where in the course of a year their ideas and commitments can be re-examined, their interests and goals allowed to take new form, and their self-awareness developed with a view to their future paths. There is no question in my mind that Danish students are able to have the kind of experience that Erikson refers to as a psychosocial moratorium - a sanctioned delay or pause between phases of the life cycle - both at the Continuation School and the Folk High School. At the former the positive experience of solidarity (together with the presence of both clear rule boundaries and significant areas of personal freedom) allows young people of 14-18 to have a year apart from everything they have known previously. It is a year which provides them with a new set of challenges and opportunities combined with a moratorium on many of the important choices and decisions they face. It is not surprising, then, that the Folk High Schools and the Continuation Schools have never been more popular than they are today in the 1990s. Both in the number of schools and in the number of students attending them, these schools are more in demand than ever before.

What happens to students, however, after the year at the Continuation School or the 6 months at a Folk High School? Is the experience something that transforms them and puts new life into them, in terms of the Grundtvigian heritage discussed earlier by Jørgen Carlsen? Do Danish students leave these schools with a sense of personal mission, as did so many of the students in the last decades of the nineteenth century? Or is it more correct to say that they are immediately swallowed up in the normative Danish secondary school world of competition, and performance in a knowledge-based school system? Does their experience of what Danes call the "folkelig" – the popular characteristics of Denmark – in these two schools come to give them a deeper commitment to the cause of life in the sense meant by N.F.S. Grundtvig and Christen Kold, the men whose lives and work gave rise to such schools, and to the independent free schools? Or is a stay at such a school merely a brief parenthesis in their busy lives as postmodern consumers in an increasingly atomized, privatized Danish society? It is impossible to give a simple yes or no answer to these questions; yet the questions are valuable because they provide some insight into the challenges faced both by these two school forms, and by Danish educational institutions in a more general sense. In conclusion, I wish to remark that I offer this brief comparative perspective not as a hard and fast conclusion, but as a basis for discussion and further reflection.

5. Being Young in a Modernist Society

Per Schultz Jørgensen

It is not so long ago that growing into adulthood simply involved the taking over an existing culture with all that it contained of knowledge, skills and norms. The tradition was there and in assuming it the individual acquired an identity. This is no longer the case. By and large the individual must now go out in search of a guiding principle and a context in which to function. How then do children manage this transition and what can school offer them of help? On the basis of recent research and through the perspective of social psychology the following chapter attempts to discuss these two central questions.

Modernist society

Society today is often given the epithet of "high-tech", "post-modern" or "information". Characteristic of it is a dynamic transformation of a hitherto unseen intensity and impact which has taken place since World War II and in particular since the 1960s. We are not speaking here of technological achievements and innovations but of cultural revolution. Traditions and stable elements in society have been weakened as the emphasis increases on transitions, changes and options for the individual. This has led to an emphasis on subjectivity and the need for each person to create meaning for themselves, to find their own red thread through life.

In this transformation we are perhaps more aware of what we are abandoning than what we are seeking – hence the prefix in "post-modern". For the break-up has simultaneous elements of both expansion and fragmentation. On the one hand we find the globalisation of information,

communication and technology, increased productivity, speed of decision, border-breaking market creations, and an explosion in picture and communication channels. A market and technological expansion that day by day breaks new ground.

On the other hand we are watching the breakdown of a whole series of fixed notions. These include the dissolving of the time-place framework and the fragmentation of our common cultural features – of values, norms and traditions. Modernity is a relativisation of central values that offer new opportunities – but only at a price. This means that children cannot simply take over a social tradition and a cultural inheritance from their parents, for neither the tradition nor the inheritance are any longer worthy of credence. Schools have given up trying to build on a generation of children with a unified culture in their schoolbags, nor can they be mediators of an authorised body of knowledge. For this simply does not exist to the same degree as before. Knowledge is not a limited unity but is coupled to an attitude, to a way of dealing with things or to a process rather than to a clearly defined ability or skill.

What then is the school's role in this modernist society? What are children to learn? How should the school mediate its knowledge when it is no longer so clear what knowledge actually is? The answer is that school has become just as much a socialising factor as a provider of knowledge. Or rather, in modern society knowledge is linked to personal acquisition of it in a new sense: as an insight created by the individual.

Thus there is no escaping a powerful el-

ement of individuality in modern society. So what do young people put into their search process? How do they understand themselves? And how does the school fit into this search?

Individuality as a search process

Children in modern Danish society are open but self-centred searchers. They are on their way towards participating in the many cultural offers available and towards realising their own potential. They do not build on fixed inner notions of frameworks and values, but are flexible and experimental. They are more outer than inner-controlled, though this does not necessarily imply insecurity and doubt. The outer control is a search process.

They grow up in a modern family where both parents are increasingly linked to the labour market and where children and adults alike see themselves in a constant chase for qualifications: in education, training, knowledge and skills. A Danish survey by E.J.Hansen in 1994 showed that parents placed the children's independence as the family's highest child-raising goal and their education as a top priority. Parents are no longer authorities as they were before in relation to older children. Today they are much more equally placed – more like in a friendship than a traditional parent-child relationship, as is clear from a 1986 survey by P.S. Jørgensen et al of the parents' role in relation to 13-15-year-old children.

So children and young people are nowadays individualists. In 1994 in the daily newspaper *Politiken*, Lars Hoppe, a young Dane spoke of his generation as being without illusions:

"Most of my generation have a sense of purpose. This is true of girls to a greater degree than of us boys. Even though today's young people are so goal-conscious, we still spend time on leisure pursuits, on jobs and on being together with one another. Young people of my age set great store on being individuals. Each of us has our own interests as regards sport, music and clothes. But even though we see ourselves as individualists, being together also plays an important role for us. Individualism is not synonymous with egoism, at least not in my generation."

A sense of purpose and personal choice. Similarly in a Dutch survey of young people (Du Bois-Raymond et al, *Life-course Transitions and the Future of Dutch Youth*, 1994) we find a change from the traditional life-cycle of school, education, pairing off and establishing themselves as adults – to a path characterised as "a biography of choices". Here the young choose a career and a path that express their attempt to create their own personal context in which to live.

The search process has to do with identity and it takes place in important arenas: among mates, in leisure-time, through the media, through cultural activities – and through school and other educational institutions. Here the individual's identity is tested, explored, reorganised, for the biography must be created by the person in question. Only he or she is responsible.

This identity is characterised as outer-controlled and searching – in a process that lasts from early childhood up into the teenage years, and which in one sense is endless, for it must be kept up in the many arenas. But what is it they are looking out for – and what actually are the educational methods available to the school?

Cultural arenas

The cultural arenas are places of activity – that is what first strikes the observer. And every survey confirms that the vast majority of children are highly extrovert and active. A 1995 Danish survey by D. Andersen shows how much children "go to things" in their leisure-time. They go to sport and they go to the movies, they go to their mates and they go to clubs and classes where they can learn to play drums, ride a horse or be a scout. In these arenas of close cameraderie a coded language is developed that both links them to one another and puts down a tentative anchor to their own identity.

In these arenas they are exposed to a huge range of influences, such as the media world of clothes and commercialisation. There is a fair deal of research to show that not even little children are immune to advertising but are swiftly trained experts in decoding TV commercials (Jørgensen, 1992). Children love the ones where something happens, where someone is funny, where there is a surprise. From as early as 7 they know the purpose of adverts and are largely sceptical of smart messages, though like all of us they are influenced by what they see. Children aged 10-12 can sense the values at work behind the commercials, while still finding it difficult to distinguish programme-length commercials, where the whole film is one long commercial, from ordinary cartoon films with no commercial link.

In general therefore children who grow up with the media-arena around them are not naive recipients but competent consumers, depending on their age, sex, social background and previous experience. They see through the message aimed at them, but can simultaneously use it in their own understanding of life. TV commercials are regarded as part of a lifestyle marked by presentation, facade, checking-out, choice, evaluation and possible incorporation. As cultural elements adverts have their own logic and can be responded to, if they are seen as user-friendly, often meaning image-friendly. In contrast to the endless round of schoolwork they can be selected or dismissed at will. And without compromising themselves schools too can offer subjects and methods that pupils can have an attitude or opinion about, something they can use in their own lives.

In his article *Mirroring meeting, mirroring media: the microphysics of reflexivity. Cultural Studies 8 (1994) pp.321-340 (1994)* J. Fornäs speaks of the cultural arenas as containing their own norms and linguistic codes, allowing the opportunity for reflecting oneself in and by others – a mirroring process known as reflexivity. Reflexivity is not necessarily an intellectual process; it can also be linked to physical activity. But in the arenas mentioned it takes place as a communicative process, as a cultural manifestation, as a media preference and as an aesthetic expression. Reflexivity is both a highly personal process and yet a social, even a group phenomenon too. In the arena young people test themselves to develop their identity and measure themselves against others.

But perhaps "identity" should be written in the plural form. For there appear to be many versions of it, which can be chosen, transformed, even dramatically staged. Identity is chosen in relation to the situation: the conscious task is to construct oneself out of the various options.

One may rightly ask whether this development is a dangerous one, or simply an extension of the personal freedom so prized in Denmark. Are we talking of progression or re-gression? As D. Kellner says:

"On the one hand it increases one's freedom to play with one's identity and change one's life dramatically (which may be good for some), while on the other hand it can lead to a totally fragmented existence subject to the whims of fashion and the subtle indoctrination of advertising and popular culture."

Lash S. & Friedman J. (eds) *Modernity & Identity (Blackwell, Oxford 1992) pp.141-177.*

A modern identity fights to create a nucleus of self-understanding while constantly risking fragmentation and lack of a personal context. The individual is deeply involved in the play and its presentation and the changes of scenery in the many arenas – all with the possible outcome of failure to create a credible context behind the external control. This risk also impinges on the school's agenda.

The central role of the school

The task of the school is to ensure that young people acquire the necessary qualifications to meet the demands of modern society. This role will be even more vital in future as the following factors come into play:

a) The education sector will expand in size, time and importance.
b) Demand will grow for qualifications, enabling the individual to compete both for the many jobs on offer and on the basis of them.
c) Equal opportunities and pay will increase so that women's role in the educational sector will grow.
d) Education will become a lifelong process.
e) The education sector will in practice have a monopoly on mediating a safe and secure society.
f) The education sector will function more and more as a sorting-system, where rejection is tantamount to dismissal into a group labelled "at risk".

The school lays the foundation for this progress through the sector – and for the later possible rejection. At the same time the children's premises for the trajectory are very different from that of their parents when they were young. This is the starting-point when considering the content of the school.

Thus the school stands at a crossroads. What shall we offer young people who will have to function as adults in a modernist society making their choices on a personal basis? How can the school become an arena that mediates not just ready-made knowledge but also personal awareness.

The school debate

Of course the question is not new. Throughout this century the contrast between the transmission of knowledge and the creation of attitudes has been debated. A trained man or a learned man, qualification or socialisation, these are still the central concepts.

From the 1960s to the 80s the discussion ebbed and flowed. Critical Marxists revealed the extent of bourgeois indoctrination, right-wing economists argued for the school's adaptation to market forces and commercial life. In between, the educational reforms have renewed the school and its purpose, emphasizing pupil participation, motivation, and experience-based learning. Groupwork and experience teaching were the keywords – active learning, holistic learning and the process approach followed in their wake. But without forming an answer to the problem of modernity outlined above.

The power-balance in the political debate on education took a swing to the right in the late 1980s. The market place, job qualification, skills acquisition, and careers guidance were in the high seat.

As the new millennium approaches, however, the market vision is fading a little. The knowledge explosion continues. Increasing demands are being made on people's own management of their options. Perhaps this is leading to a reconciliation of opposites, with the trained man leaning towards the learned woman and the qualified woman working alongside the socialised man.

En route to a new school

What to teach is nowadays inseparable from modernist society. The rapid obsolescence of knowledge prevents us from even using "information" as a buzzword. It is no use just updating the curriculum, for the information society has demonstrably succeeded in setting its own limit: worthless knowledge.

The choice of curriculum content is also fraught with difficulty. Old-style objectivity and ultimate truth have given way to relativism, utilitarianism and flexible adaptation to the demands of the moment. And so the teacher's role as an authority is changing into one of mediator, coordinator and credible role-model for the pupil.

The inevitable consequence of these conditions can be formulated into the concept of a new school that underlines the pupils' personal control of the learning process, much as they learn to master a computer. For it is not just a question of making a learning process pupil-centred, but of the production of knowledge and its influence on the education process.

The challenge can be formulated thus: the regulation of knowledge cannot be definitively fixed by external authorities – knowledge as insight and awareness must be constructed in a process where the pupil is made responsible. It is a question of the degree of pupil autonomy in the production of knowledge or a weighting of the self-controlling as opposed to the teacher-controlling element in learning.

The school will then become a particular socio-cultural arena that can offer youngsters a cultural feedback, not alongside the learning process which the school must continue to champion, but as an element within it. The paradigm can be formulated as a contrast between Information on the one hand and Knowledge on the other.

In our discussions of school and learning we often include these dimensions, well knowing that in our context they cannot compete with the offers from the surrounding market. We can do something else, however, which has much more to do with the personal element. How then does the school tackle this point?

It seems to me that the among other things it must come from valuing children's own experience somewhat higher. They cannot take over the teacher's perception of yesterday's world, and they cannot build on values that are no longer seen as valid. Nor can they manage with a fingertip knowledge that proves to be out

Information	Knowledge
offer	content
quantity	quality
activity as a goal in itself	activity as a means to something else
reproduction	production
cleverness	reflection/mirroring
skill	competence

of touch with the modernist reality. They must therefore be made co-responsible for the learning they are in the midst of. This takes place in a productive process in which they create their own experiences. In other words, they will build on a concept of knowledge that does not emphasize the amount of information, but what they do with it: selecting, evaluating and constructing a new understanding. From knowledge as information to knowledge as proficiency.

In this proficiency process youngsters are given a response to themselves as people, being faced with a demand for responsibility, immersion and consistency. Herein lies the opportunity for an education that takes place through the learning process, not alongside it.

The teacher of today has a social and psychological task of huge dimensions. It is not enough just to pass on the basis he or she has learned, which will be out of date in a few years. Nor will it help to pour information into pupils who are already faced with the problem of gaining an overview. Instead the teacher must teach the pupil to choose. He or she must develop a confidence in them so that they can utilize the proficiency that they acquire. The teacher must therefore arrange situations that constructively present the pupils with meaningful challenges, teaching them the necessity of choice and the consequence of action. The teacher cannot do this as an information expert but by becoming a lively participant and acting as a credible, integrated, reflective person. Only then is the teacher able to challenge the pupils to understand themselves and move on in their own process.

The teacher's qualification is therefore of a deeply human nature. This is where the challenge to modernity lies and its built-in threat not only of superficiality, but also its possible perspective in the direction of the divided, fragmented personality.

We are on the way to a new vison of school and learning. Perhaps only as small steps at this point, but steps that can be observed as an experiment and developmental work in many places in the Danish school system over the coming years.

Under all circumstances there is a growing recognition of the need to develop new learning environments for people of all ages – children, youngsters, the middle-aged and the elderly. This will not happen just as a reaction to a professional and technically accentuated need for qualifications. It is also an answer to the challenges that a modernist society faces and with a perspective in the direction of reflection, personal skill and competence.

6. Culture and Education – 16 to 19

Hanna Broadbridge

Education and the educated person

In the Danish concepts of *dannet* and *uddannet* lies a play on words that is difficult to reproduce in English, since both in a sense mean educated.

Dannet means formed or adapted and assumes a model towards which one strives. It also means grown together with or developed. In this sense it can be applied to the individual who has grown together with society, and to society which has developed the individual. The concept covers an understanding of one's own and other cultures as well as a degree of self-awareness. The nearest English equivalent is "educated" in the somewhat old-fashioned sense of an "educated" person. i.e. someone who is well-read, who has a social position and cares for the social graces.

uddannet on the other hand means trained in a particular skill or skills. To achieve this one has learned to appropriate a subject matter, analyse a problem, raise and test a hypothesis, reach a conclusion, and apply the result to a further purpose, possibly even to another subject area. One has acquired skills, multi-disciplinary knowledge and self-awareness, and one is ready to apply them. The nearest English equivalent is "trained", as in he is a trained architect.

Philosophy of life

For the last English essay before their final examinations recently a Danish Gymnasium class of 18/19-year-olds were given 3 weeks to write an essay on their philosophy of life. After a week there was general panic. What sort of a question was that? How should they tackle it? What was the teacher after? Accordingly another lesson was spent with the teacher, who explained that they were simply to write down their beliefs, their values, the way they approached life, their thoughts on its significance or lack of it, their purpose in life, perhaps even the meaning of life in general, or at least of their own. No one then protested that this was unreasonable; in fact they clearly thought this could be interesting. Nor was it considered a hindrance that they would have to write in a foreign language, albeit one they were well trained in.

The teacher was surprised at the results. Many had given up on the subject, had nevertheless been unable to define the question and therefore the answer. It proved difficult to summarize the effects of three formative years in school or to describe the values on which they would build their lives. Instead many had simply outlined their dreams and expectations – a year abroad, further education, a job, a husband or wife, a house, children etc. When the teacher questioned their lack of a philosophy to underpin their dreams, the class cheerfully admitted the superficiality of much of their lives but then sat quietly and thoughtfully – partly ashamed, partly intrigued – as the subject was developed.

The story illustrates the difference between educated and trained in the senses used above. Young people on the threshold of tertiary education have become very much aware of how the world works, but have little desire and even less time to reflect on their view of it or their place in it. They are certainly trained, but are they educated?

Somersaults

For centuries Denmark was educated through books. The older one grew, the more these books were allowed to be discussed rather than just digested. Philosophical thoughts and concepts were absorbed and became part of oneself, so educated people lived on the basis of the Bible and the great philosophers, poets and scientists.

Over the past 50 years the value of such an education has been called into question by politicians, economists and ideologues looking for professional skills and specialisation to secure for society an expertise that could be swiftly transformed into jobs and money. In a rapidly changing world commercially useful subjects came to the fore.

More and more 16-year-olds began to opt for tertiary education, in Technical, Commercial or the more academic Gymnasium. The last-mentioned in particular experienced a rise in numbers. In the 1960s the Gymnasium (offering a 3-year course for 16 to 19-year-olds) admitted only 10% of a year. With the addition of HF, the Higher Preparatory Course, a similar 2-year course introduced in 1967 and often sited at a Gymnasium, this figure had risen to 46% by the mid-1990s. The remaining 54% attend vocational schools: the Technical Schools now account for 26% and the Commercial Schools for 25% of a school year; a further 1.5% go to Agricultural Schools, while courses for the social and health services take 1.4%.

Back in the 1960s the politicians realised that the commercial and social future of the country could only be secured by raising the level of training for the advanced jobs that demanded a solid basis of knowledge coupled with a creative approach to new ideas and an awareness of their practical consequences. The 1960s saw a reform of the entire educational system, bringing greater access to tertiary training, new curricula and syllabi, and a higher professional status for teachers. At the lower levels child-centred education and an emphasis on personal social development increased both the pupils' sense of security and the teachers' workload. The gap between teacher knowledge and pupil ignorance narrowed as pupils moved on to first-name terms with their teachers and the individual child's potential was explored. With liberal values in the ascendant the Danes believed for 20 years or so that they were at the forefront of educational and social development.

Until, that is, the realisation dawned in the late 1980s that a generation of self-centred pupils had grown up which in its teenage years was throwing out the carefully inculcated concept of social solidarity in the rush to grab the cake and eat it. Everyone wanted to be an architect or a midwife. As unemployment swept across Europe and social currents outside the classroom put pressure on schools, the weakest pupils went on the dole or to the wall. The unrivalled education system began to reveal its flaws as too many school-leavers demonstrated a lack of basic skills and a disregard for social culture. The hour of self-examination had arrived. Was the pupil's freedom and well-being now taking priority over actual learning? Had teachers become reserve parents and psychologists rather than mediators of knowledge and skills? International reports and comparisons in the early 1990s revealed weak spots in the Danish system, not least with regard to reading ability.

The dream of tertiary education for all dissolved as the economy took a downturn in the 1970s and political signals changed from green to red. Requirements for entry into tertiary education were tightened and competition for university places intensified. With the Gymnasium and HF promoting intellectual values and personal choice to an ever-increasing number of youngsters, society was failing to attract school-leavers into production. New technology put people out of work, and sadly the centuries-old system of apprenticeships had to be severely curtailed. Denmark's famed social network was stretched to breaking-point.

Again there was a national somersault. In the early 1980s young people began to think less in terms of intellectual achievement and more about marketing their talents economically. This meant learning specific skills, particularly within technology. The successful whizz-kids moved into the fast lane, and within five years of leaving school were earning more than their teachers. Although they were relatively few, they were setting the pace. Public success was admired in a chaotic, fragmented world where personal and social security were no longer guaranteed.

And yet. However much their profiles were admired they were not especially envied. Down-to-earth most Danish youngsters remained, seeking a deeper satisfaction and a broader life-base. As the economy gradually gathered speed, the trend in the 1990s was still towards a general education, giving access to all kinds of tertiary education. The Gymnasium and HF offer a more culturally orientated course, including a heavier emphasis on cultural subjects such as Danish literature, History, Classical Culture, and Religious Studies, and creative subjects like Art, Music and Drama. The Commercial and Technical Schools also give access to tertiary education but require a more specific planning of the course.

The explanations for this development are many: 16-year-olds are not yet ready to choose a particular career, nor to relinquish the cultural and creative subjects that fill much of their lives both in and out of school; before making their choice they need more time to look realistically at their own qualities and skills and to take responsibility for themselves. In the light of the new Europe and with the world as a global village they seek a deeper understanding of their own cultural roots.

At the same time their teenage years are not only years of school and homework, projects and examinations; they are also a time of commitment and consumption. For the majority of pupils this means a part-time job with some of the wages being spent at the weekend. They argue that it gives experience of a different kind from study and that they get to know other people and the demands of a workplace, including punctuality and responsibility. Many teachers on the other hand believe that the pupils' schoolwork is correspondingly weaker, and have to weigh up their roles as teacher and guide with those of judge and jury.

Choice of school at 16

When pupils at the age of 16 choose one of the three main courses of education, Gymnasium, Commercial School or Technical School, most of them consider their own interest and ability as the primary criteria. Parents and teachers are also involved in the decision, which is made chiefly on the basis of results achieved during the final year of the Folkeskole, but partly also on their own interest as well as on job prospects via further education. Only very few can find a traditional apprenticeship, while another small group, often of pupils tired of "school" can pursue their education completely outside the normal system. On these new Free Youth Training (FUU), young people can put together their own education through activities under the guidance of a study leader.

But for 95% of 16/17-year-olds the doors of the new school open every August. Inside are new surroundings, friends and teachers, new subjects, demands and methods, greater independence, opportunity and responsibility, but also greater confusion, uncertainty and pressure. The vast majority manage the transition with ease, but in the course of the first few months there is a drop-out rate of 2% for the Gymnasium, 4% for the Commercial Schools and 9% for the Technical Schools. Over the full course these figures rise to 3%, 11% and 25% respectively. Reasons for dropping out range from the school's social life and attitudes over learning demands and own inabilities to dislike of teachers and own immaturity.

All three school forms have common features and common subject content, including Danish and foreign languages, but levels of competence vary, and subject content follows to some extent the form indicated in the school's name: academic, commercial or technical.

The Gymnasium – 3 years

35% of a given year choose the Gymnasium, a figure that is slowly but surely rising. Around 60% of these are now girls. Before entrance a choice has been made to take options within the natural sciences or the humanities. There is a joint curriculum through the school for many subjects, but syllabi may differ here. Danish and History, for example, have the same syllabus on the science as well as the humanities line, but in the final year of English Shakespeare is optional for the former and compulsory for the latter.

The first year comprises 9 general subjects with an average of 4 periods a week of 45 minutes. In the second year 2 or 3 options replace subjects finished after the first year. In the third and final year new subjects and new options become available. All in all roughly half the entire course contains compulsory subjects and half optional subjects.

Over the three years pupils become increasingly responsible for their own learning. In both oral and written work a high standard of independent and critical thought is expected through an interactive dialogue with the teacher and classmates. Such interaction has long been a central pillar of Danish education in the belief that intellectual challenge stimulates individual and social responsibility. This can only be achieved if the pupils feel free to create ideas, formulate and deliver them, and hear them challenged in open discussion.

Another key feature of all schools at this level is the freedom within limits for teachers and pupils to decide their own curricula. Thus the third-year English class must study a Shakespeare play, but *which* Shakespeare play is left to them and their teacher to decide. The widely-read teacher and the well-stocked bookroom can offer on average 5 different plays, and a show of pupils' hands will decide that this year *Macbeth* is preferred to *Hamlet, Prince of Denmark*. Likewise, methodology is left to the teacher and the class, as is evaluation of the course on completion. Pupil participation in this democratic process makes great demands on the teacher but offers the equally great reward of genuine commitment from decentralised decision-making.

Many subjects have a historical slant while incorporating the latest thinking in the area. A focus on international developments and new ethical dilemmas, combined with the wide range of subjects and methods, is one of the great strengths of the Gymnasium. Conversely it is also one of its weaknesses, for pupils are required to know a lot about a lot and naturally their preferences shine through as the course progresses. The individual subjects and lessons are barely related to one another and pupils end up with an encyclopaedic knowledge, lots of views on lots of subjects but, as the initial anecdote illustrated, no coherent philosophy of life.

The individual pupil's knowledge, working methods and maturity are tested to the full in the special self-chosen written

Thoughts from 1g to 3g at Aalborghus Gymnasium
Trine Christensen

I look back on my best summer so far,
the summer I left Folkeskole behind.
At first I went round with a strange empty feeling,
everything new was about to begin.

Old friends turned up again in Gymnasium.
Curiosity blossomed for the town's nightlife;
"shops and town trips" were viewed with new eyes,
new friendships put down their first strong roots.

Now summer is over, the friends still hold fast;
the holiday, in which everything blossomed
and I used up one whole film in a week,
will be remembered as one great leap.

That's 1g, now I'm a veteran 3g,
two years older and changing my ways.
The school that was foreign has now become mine,
a part of me to be always recalled.

I now know more about Homer and Piaf
than in 1g, but also how
the world ought to look. Automatically
school brought new interests, particular views.

Gymasium is over all too soon,
summers improve as I move on and up;
new friends turn into inseparable buddies,
teachers' oddities become our own.

For me Aalborghus has been a fixed point,
When I finish my finals, much will change.
I'll enjoy my last days at school to the full,
for before I've noticed, they're gone for good.

study produced each year after a period of research and analysis. Since its introduction in 1989, following its success as an important element of the HF course, it has reflected the demands of further education, society and business life for independence and analysis.

Throughout the three years pupils are continuously assessed in both oral and written disciplines. Classroom competition is not so much against one another as towards the grades required by tertiary education in a particular subject. At the end of each school year there are written examinations in major subjects and locally controlled oral examinations in which teachers act as external examiners for each other's pupils. All pupils bar a tiny minority pass the final examinations; it is their grades, together with their continual assessment grades, that decide their future.

HF – the Higher Preparatory Course – 2 years

In the 1960s it became clear that a group of adults who had missed out on further education in the post-war years were pressing for the opportunity to join the rapidly expanding job market, particularly in the middle range of skills. The HF course introduced in 1967 to meet these needs was an original and exciting concept, offering a 2-year full-time general education somewhat on the lines of the Gymnasium to adults whose qualifications included experience and maturity. A high degree of self-motivation and independence was expected and achieved, and a wide range of people from all corners of the country qualified themselves for further education as teachers, nurses and in some cases university-trained professionals. As these reserves began to run dry, younger pupils, often direct from the Folkeskole, replaced them, and in many places the course has had to adapt to a less mature and less motivated clientele.

Since HF also gives access to tertiary education and since its teachers are trained to the same professional standard as the Gymnasium, the subject content, teaching and assessment methods and final examinations are very similar. The distinguishing feature of HF used to be its theme-orientation and independent experience, but these have now been adopted by the Gymnasium too. The social life of HF pupils was much less linked to the class and the school, since they came from a wider range of age and background – in the early days a retired blacksmith could be found sitting next to a 20-year-old mother. Teachers developed new methods to meet pupil (and ministerial) expectations, and many of these were later transferred to the Gymnasium.

Like the Gymnasium, HF is financed by the county; the few courses that are private or linked to teacher training colleges receive some state funding. However, the educational responsibility for both lies with the Ministry of Education. Representatives from the local area sit on the governors' committee responsible for major decisions affecting the school. The day-to-day running is in the hands of the principal.

Teaching is free; books and study materials are loaned to the pupils for the duration of their stay. Staff in both the Gymnasium and HF have trained at university for 6 years with a major subject (4 years) and a minor one (2 years), both of which they teach. With the gradual increase in numbers they have had to adapt their academic criteria to a much wider range of pupils. One important difference from the Gymnasium is that HF students stand or fall on their examination grades at the end of the 2 years – there is no continual assessment grade, although students are of course informed of their situation on a regular basis, and the introduction of some form of continual assessment grade is under consideration.

The HF "Sweeper"
- Peter Kuhlman, Frederiksborg Gymnasium, Hillerød.

Charlotte's father had always said that she was stupid. In 9th class she smoked hash, went shoplifting and burgled local summer homes with her mates. Then one day she changed her ways and started at the local education centre. She passed her exams, and decided on the HF course. Since her father still thought she was stupid, she had to forge his signature on her application. She passed with flying colours and wrote to her teachers:

"I know that I became another person in those 2 years. It was as if everything I had believed gradually faded as the knowledge I was acquiring forced me to think about my view of the world in a new way. I feel you gave me a new world and a great self-confidence to put into it."

Caroline is 26 and has a child of 2. In her 2nd HF year she is pregnant again – with twins. The birth is due in between her scheduled oral exams in Social Studies and Psychology. One morning she calls the school and asks if she can move her exams from the afternoon to the morning because the hospital wants to induce the birth on Monday afternoon. She has persuaded the hospital to wait until after lunch so she can do her Social Studies exam. Later in the week, she says, she'll be ready for the Psychology if someone can look after the twins during the exam.

Two authentic stories from everyday life at an HF centre in Hillerød, north of Copenhagen. HF attracts young people who were not born with a silver spoon in their mouths and the Danish Encyclopedia on their bookshelves. They would not feel so at home elsewhere in the education system as in this "sweeper" course, which brings together a diversified group of young people and gives them a broad education, of-ten against the odds. The 2-year course qualifies them for further study, including university, and it is constantly under review to adapt itself to this special group of youngsters – and occasional mature students.

Charlotte and Caroline are typical of the many young people who challenge sometimes difficult conditions and win through to a higher level of training and education.

Student Democracy
- Solana Larsen, Nørre Gymnasium

Student democracy is generally regarded as a Good Thing by teachers and students alike, yet it is often difficult to get students to take it seriously – and equally hard to get teachers and leaders to listen to student voices. Some see a student council as just another weight on the bureaucratic scales.

A well-run student council can benefit the school environment tremendously, however, working primarily as an organ of communication to provide running criticism, praise and discussion on school life. It creates greater understanding between all sides and allows the students to feel more a part of the school than a product of it.

Students have just as strong opinions about day-to-day life at the school as everyone else. Do not expect anyone to express their opinion without there being a purpose behind it.

At many Gymnasiums students spend hours discussing what colour the toilet paper should be – without reaching a result! They are not necessarily less brainy than those who seek to cooperate with the school leaders about improving school structures, or those who discuss changing the national policy on Gymnasiums while juggling with limited funds. The toilet-paper talkers are simply short of stimuli from the rest of the school: their problem is one of inspiration and responsibility. At this stage it is vital that the school leaders give them areas of responsibility to get their teeth into. At other times it is the students who should pump life into the school. All students should be constantly reminded that they have a vote. They should create activity and change in the dusty corners of their institution.

Even if you get the balance right, it is difficult to keep. A student council suffers from regular withdrawals and replacements, making its structures and methods different from year to year. A good student council rarely lasts more than a couple of years. The student year that gives most support is the one that that has something to fight for. The school must recognize this, meaning not that things should be made harder for the student council, but on the contrary, that areas of responsibility should not be taken away from the council just because there is low activity.

Some schools maintain their democracy through a representative structure, others prefer basis democracy, or a student council of 70 members with a full mandate. Some serve as a school dance committee or as the editorial board of the school newsletter. One thing is certain: the students' right to be consulted is what they themselves make of it. The wisest heads will make it a priority.

The Vocational Schools:

a) The Commercial School –
4 years

The Commercial Schools offer a broad education aimed at business life and the service industries including both practical and theoretical functions. In recent years the Commercial Schools have extended their range of subjects and widened their appeal so that about 25% of a given year now choose this option.

Historically the Commercial Schools were a supplement to the practical training of the workplace and were attended after working hours. But as demand grew for broader knowledge and more specific skills, the workplaces could no longer cope and the Commercial Schools came into being, under strong influence from local business. Nowadays expertise is required at such a depth that not all Commercial Schools offer the same subjects, but six areas are commonly taught and give access to tertiary education: office, sales, display, wholesale, finance and informatics. Within these there are further options as well as specialist areas, while school can also be attended full-time or part-time in connection with a job.

In a few places it is still possible to find traditional apprenticeships, but most businesses, institutions and organisations choose to train their staff at Commercial Schools while doing trainee service at the workplace. This is partly due to the wish to secure a reasonably high general level of education, particularly in the light of the rapid changes in society and thus commercial life.

The course model offers a basic education followed by an interaction between practical trainee service and school for a 3-year period. Further specialisation takes place in the fourth year. The general lines are determined by the Ministry of Education while the specific demands are drawn up by the teachers' professional associations. Since the clientele are young people in education there is an emphasis on personal development and an understanding of society, coupled with a breadth of knowledge that will give access to tertiary education. Four areas are therefore covered:

1) Basic subjects – giving general qualifications
2) Area subjects – offering specific subjects
3) Special subjects – ensuring a high commercial level
4) Optional subjects – providing specialisation

Among the Basic subjects are Danish and English, which are regarded as essential for every educational course in Denmark. In general the subjects offered are skills-oriented and to a lesser degree designed to develop personality or encourage creative work, but a number of new subjects and methods have been introduced to encourage pupils to develop their strengths and work on their weaknesses. Again the emphasis is on responsibility, independence and cooperation skills. Philosophy and Psychology are options in the Gymnasium, HF, and the Commercial School as are Media Studies and Gymnastics/Sport, but the Commercial School is alone in offering environmental studies, design and culture. These are available right from the start and can be adapted to particular areas of commerce and trade. such as export, information technology, marketing, economics or the financial sector. At some of the larger Commercial Schools there is an international line focussing on major languages, cultural understanding, international marketing etc., with a stay abroad as part of the course.

This development is a response to greater demand for flexibility and cultural awareness amid fierce international competition. It is not enough to learn a foreign language: you must also learn the culture in which it is spoken and how to do business in it. So shared experiences, interests, knowledge and problems are also part of business life. These are learned through simulation, realistic group and project work and theme courses so that the pupil is prepared for the stay abroad and for independent work.

Only a tiny minority leave Commercial School with just the basic course behind them; the vast majority stay on and move via the final examination to tertiary education. All Commercial Schools offer special courses to update knowledge and skills, often on request from the business world, while a number of them have courses on leadership and sports training and management.

Teachers come from various sectors of society; some are university-trained, others come from the School of Economics and Business Administration, and a few come out of business life and teach while doing supplementary teacher training. Their educational goals are to to transmit knowledge, to develop the individual and generally to prepare pupils for commercial life. The schools are self-owning and receive some state finance but have to acquire further funding by running courses or through support from local business to keep abreast of developments particularly in informatics and computer science.

In recent years numbers applying have fallen slightly partly due to the difficulty of finding trainee practice opportunities, partly to the reduction in jobs available and partly to the relatively high employment. Perhaps a further contributing factor is the preference of more pupils to pursue their personal and cultural goals through the Gymnasium.

The internationalisation of Danish society is also reflected in the rapid growth in international exchanges, supported by the European Union among others. Here both education and training come together, providing a major motivator in a number of subjects and adding a powerful, practical and ethical element to the considerable theory that has to be absorbed.

b) The Technical School – 4 years

Around 26% of 16-year-olds choose the Technical Schools, some for the basic technical education with a view to the labour market, others for the chance to move on to a more theoretical tertiary education.

Like the Commercial Schools the Technical Schools came into being to teach theory and skills in specific subjects to blue-collar workers after working hours. Every Technical School is closely linked to the local commercial structure and trains its pupils with this in mind. The schools are thus dif-

ferent from place to place, so much so in fact that part of the basic education is only available at certain schools in the country.

The tremendous range of subjects on offer includes training for the iron and metal industries, building and construction, mechanics, agriculture, catering and hair styling. One can become a graphic artist, an optician, a butcher, a baker or a candlestick maker by beginning with a basic general education followed by increasing specialisation over the 4 years. The basis is Danish, Maths and foreign languages, usually with a technical slant, as well as more theoretical subjects such as knowledge of materials and workshop techniques; after this the pupil goes to a local firm to train, returning to the school for new courses and more advanced knowledge. As with the Commercial School there are four areas of study:

1) Basic subjects – giving general qualifications
2) Area subjects – offering specific subjects
3) Special subjects – ensuring a high technical level
4) Optional subjects – providing specialisation

Practical skills are of the highest importance, but there is also great emphasis on their wider application: on development and leadership, planning, quality control, economy and marketing. To this end the teaching of theory and technique at the school is directly linked to the reality of the workplace in the world outside. Training ends with the pupil producing a practical project with professionals judging its quality. This may range from a particular kind of staircase, a jewel made of specific materials or a dinner with particular ingredients, to a hairstyle from an earlier age.

Technical School teachers can have very different backgrounds, from the academic to the craftsman, but the former must have trained in a particular subject and the latter must acquire supplementary teaching skills. Increasingly they are required to help in the personal development of their pupils, which comes not only with the courses outlined above but through subjects such as psychology, multi-media studies, and personal care.

Lack of jobs in recent years has meant lack of trainee places, so schools have been forced to do practical training within their own four walls, but with more jobs now becoming available and fewer youngsters chasing them the prospects are improving for trainee places. The schools also have a superstructure of specialised studies to meet the latest demands from business life and the workshop. These can be specifically related to a trade but may also involve subjects such as cultural knowledge or a particular foreign language. The European Union has provided the Technical Schools with considerable resources for exchange programmes and study trips, since it is in the late teenage years that inter-European awareness is created.

The Technical Schools are self-owning institutions but receive state grants and economic support from local business, which is also involved in planning course content within the framework laid down by the Ministry of Education.

dannet and uddannet

To return to the original distinction between *dannet* (formed, developed) and *uddannet* (trained, skilled) it should by now be clear that schools strive for both throughout the period in question. Where *dannet* previously meant "educated" and was applied mainly to the bourgeoisie or middle-class, it has more recently come to include knowing one's roots and one's culture, being aware of one's surroundings at home and abroad. A major element in *dannet* is therefore respect for and understanding of others.

uddannet on the other hand now means knowledge and skills, multi-disciplinary insight and the ability to analyse and conclude. Teaching strives for the most part to make the pupil *uddannet* in the belief that given the right methodology and classroom democracy the pupil will become *dannet* in the process. Teachers themselves, most of whom trained in the 1960s and 1970s when to be *dannet* meant to be a snob, have tried to avoid the word while still pursuing a 1990s version of the concept. Many youngsters, feeling their lack of roots, of history, of Danish culture, are open to teachers willing to equip them with these essentials, particularly in the Gymnasium and HF.

Whatever their choice of school Danish youngsters share the belief of the romantic age in learning through travel, not only within Europe – where Interrail is very popular – but further afield, particularly after their final examinations. Large numbers of youngsters spend a year abroad, experiencing foreign cultures and discovering their own level of maturity, testing in practice their beliefs in tolerance and respect, and gaining a perspective on the formative influences of home and school. Another popular option after final examinations, and one very much in keeping with the Danish cultural tradition is to spend 6 months or so at one of the 100 or so Folk High Schools around the country. Here in a wide range of discussions and activities they learn their strengths and discover new talents in a lively atmosphere of commitment and solidarity.

The ability to relate to one's surroundings critically – positively and negatively – to recognise strengths and weaknesses in oneself, and to pursue goals that are personally and perhaps also socially rewarding if not now then later – these are the characteristics of most Danish youngsters on the completion of their secondary education. Meanwhile society awaits them with its demands for commitment to work, political involvement, economic contribution and cultural activity, and not least for flexibility. There is no product at the end of the three or four years, but the process has been all-important.

Act on the Upper Secondary School (Gymnasium) 1990

1. (1) In continuation of the 9th form of the Folkeskole the Gymnasium offers continued general education of 3 years' duration which shall provide students with the necessary basis for further studies concluding with an examination, the Studentereksamen, which qualifies students for admission to further and higher education.

2. (1) The teaching in the Gymnasium shall be offered in 2 separate lines: the Languages line and the Mathematics line.
(2) Subject to certain variations between the 2 lines teaching shall be offered in the following subjects: Biology, Business Economics, Chemistry, Classical Studies, Computer Science, Danish, Design, Drama, English, Film/TV Studies, French, German, Geography, Classical Greek, History, Italian, Latin, Mathematics, Music, Natural Sciences, Physical Education and Sport, Physics, Religious Studies, Russian, Social Studies, Spanish, Technical Studies, Visual Arts. The students shall also be offered vocational and educational guidance.

8. (1) The county council shall decide on matters relating to:

1) The allocation of grants to the Gymnasia within its county and the financial framework of the individual schools.

2) The appointment of school principals, after the Ministry of Education has recognized the applicants' qualifications.

3) The appointment and dismissal of teachers and other staff, after the principal's recommendation.

4) Special needs education etc.

10. (1) The Gymnasia shall set up a school board, comprising representives of the county council, the municipal or local district councils in the local area, parents, staff and students of the school. The staff and student representatives must not represent a majority on the board. The school principal shall sit in a non-voting capacity.

(2) The composition, manner of election and competence of the board shall appear from the statutes of the school, which shall be laid down by the county council.

(3) The board shall – on the recommendation of the principal – fix the maximum number of students in the individual classes, the subjects to be offered, and the holiday plan. The board shall furthermore be responsible for the cooperation between the school and the home. It shall contribute to the solution of social tasks in relation to the school, lay down the rules of conduct for the school, participate in building matters, and may make proposals to the county council concerning the improvement of buildings etc.

(4) The board shall – on the recommendation of the principal and within the budgetary framework laid down by the county council – fix the budget of the school.

12. (1) The principal shall be in charge of the day-to-day management of the school and shall be responsible to the county council for the activities of the school.

examinations.

(2) The principal shall be responsible for the educational aspects of the teaching and examinations at the school to the Minister of Education and Research.

(3) The principal shall supervise and distribute the work among the staff of the school and make all concrete decisions concerning the students of the school.

(4) The principal shall be responsible for examinations and certification.

13. (1) Each Gymnasium shall set up a teachers' council consisting of the principal and all the teachers.

(2) The teachers' council shall act as advisor to the principal.

(3) The teachers' council shall lay down its own procedures and elect its own chair.

14. (1) Each Gymnasium shall set up a students' council, elected by the students.

(2) The students' council shall submit its opinions to the principal, including on general matters relating to students' conditions.

15. (1) The Minister of Education and Research shall have overall responsibility for and shall supervise the teaching and examinations of the Gymnasium.

(2) The Minister of Education and Research may give instructions to the principal on educational matters and lay down regulations pertaining to complaints about and repeal of decisions taken in connection with

(3) The Minister of Education may request the necessary information about the schools and arrange visits to the schools.

7. The Danish Gymnasium from a German Perspective

Jutta Rüdiger

After some 10 years teaching at upper secondary level and working as an administrator with the School Supervisory Authority in Germany, I regard teaching in a Danish Gymnasium as an enjoyable and stimulating experience. Both in teaching and in observing my surroundings I have acquired an insight into the educational system of another country.

Informality

Entering a Danish Gymnasium as a German used to particular cultural traditions and hierarchic structures, I find procedures here appear to be very informal and unauthoritarian, with equally effective work and good results. Informality being a general trait of Danish society, it can be encountered on many levels of school life. It is revealed not only in the familiar form of address by first names between staff and students and the use of the informal second person singular ("du" as opposed to "De", even to the Minister of Education!) but also in the very casual dress code of the school staff. This informality is also regarded as an expression of the ideal of equality and democracy in the daily cooperation of the groups involved. Mutual respect and a staunch trust in the individual's will to channel his or her abilities properly create a pleasantly relaxed work atmosphere and a personal feeling of freedom, thus opening up for commitment and experimentation without the tight framework of bureaucratic control.

Staff-student relations

It is this atmosphere that I feel is the most conspicuous element in Danish school life, and its consequences become evident in the fact that students are represented on all school committees as equal partners. In the classroom itself visiting German students from partner schools have often marvelled at the very personal, relaxed student-teacher relationship and revised their preconceived idea of potential abuse of the familiar form of address. Using the teacher's first names does not result in undue fraternization or lack of respect, but rather allows for a secure sense of community in a given work situation. Authority is thus seen and felt as more a matter of personality and professional expertise than formal status.

This attitude also influences the general tone of the school. A calm and friendly, essentially benevolent way of expressing oneself is favoured by all, whereas there is a distinct aversion to aggressive behaviour or authoritarian orders. This makes daily school life smooth enough - though at times it gives rise to the suspicion of some underlying fear of conflict and open confrontation. Students in particular find it hard to meet harsher conditions in a broad understanding of the word, be this a sharper tone or higher demands on the quality of their performance. I sometimes wonder if this difficulty is a flip-side consequence of the Danish welfare state: an increasing number of people lack the spirit of "fight" and competition, but instead expect immediate support and "fair" treatment in a world of fewer chances and tougher challenges.

I have often found that Danish students lack this healthy aggressiveness in the sense of defying temporary odds and handling defeats. They seem to expect somebody else to take responsibility and smoothe things over for them. This attitude might also be a result of 9-10 long years in the Folkeskole, which in many cases does not adequately equip school-leavers with the necessary tools to cope with both intellectual and personal challenges. The transition to the more demanding Gymnasium is a shock for a number of 1st-year students and it takes a considerable while to adjust, an ineffective use of time for what is an intensive 3-year course. German students, starting the Gymnasium in 5th class follow a more consistent line of progress up to 11th class (corresponding to the Danish 1st-year Gymnasium), learning to cope with various methods and demands as they meet them.

Freedom to experiment

I mentioned earlier the freedom that is widely granted both students and teachers in the organization of their daily work. If administered responsibly, this possibility of defining one's own space is very fruitful: I have never before experienced colleagues with such a strong interest in questions of teaching methods and pedagogy, nor a corresponding enthusiasm for classroom experiments and cooperation on common projects. I see this openness as a tremendous inspiration for my daily work with my classes, a rewarding experience both personally and professionally. Each school year there are new ideas or promising trends discussed in our professional journals and on in-service courses, and consequently in the staff room. There is always a group of teachers burning to try new things and share failures. Against this of course, we must not forget the implications of a quite flat hierarchy with only few chances of promotion.

This lively spirit of the large group of engaged teachers is spread to the students, who are granted a similar range of possibilities to handle assignments, and at times come up with astonishing results. I feel that in this area more freedom is given to the students' creativity in individual and in group work than in Germany. This freedom, however, is radically limited by the format of the final examinations, which are centrally designed and rather inflexible compared to the daily work. The creativity practised there is not adequately matched in the final round, nor is the preparation for the written examinations, which is mostly set as homework in the form of past exam papers – a hopelessly repetitive pattern.

Homework and textbooks

It was also new to me to learn of the high percentage of students who work after school-hours, in odd jobs that help them finance their personal needs or entertainments: pocket-money is not such a self-evident matter as in Germany. In this way the young people learn at an early age to take responsibility in the outside world and to appreciate the value of work and money. But quite clearly these part-time jobs are detrimental to their school work, and are at times taken even more seriously than school itself. There is little time left to do homework and to get reasonably prepared for the next day. As a teacher one feels that the entire learning process has to be compressed into the 45 or 90 minutes of a lesson, which weighs all too heavily on the improvement of the students' performances and the educational objectives on the whole.

In contrast to Germany, students never buy any of their textbooks in Denmark, but borrow them from the school for the time of their classroom use. The idea behind this custom is once again equal opportunity. True enough, and it also facilitates procedures, as everyone in class has the book in question at the same time. Apart from a difficult delivery control, the flip-side is the official prohibition of "working" with the books in the sense of filling in exercises, underlining, making notes in the margin, revising material the following year, etc. Particularly in Languages and Literature, this restriction hampers meaningful practice and text Comprehension. What is more the school's budget (as limited as everywhere else) is enormously burdened by these expenses. Consequently, the updating of the stock is constantly a matter of fiery debate and economic controversy. Proper education cannot be "free" of costs. It would be better if the politicians responsible were more aware of the real costs of their idealistic social concepts and saw the urgency of setting clear educational priorities.

Enjoyment of school life

Let me conclude with an interesting finding. 1995 saw a comprehensive study of European students' enjoyment of their school life. Denmark occupied the top position. However, the study did not include a comparison of academic achievement or future chances of employment.

8. The Folk High School – Freedom and the Living Conversation

Jørgen Carlsen

The first Folk High School (*Folke-højskole*) in Denmark opened its doors on November 7, 1844. There are now around 100 Folk High Schools. They are often just referred to as High Schools, and should not be confused with the Folkeskole, the general, state or private comprehensive schools attended by all pupils from 6 to 16.

The 100 or so Folk High Schools around the country are for people aged 18 and upwards. With one exception they are all boarding schools. The subjects on offer are not so different from those already studied in the other areas of the education system: literature, history, psychology, ecology, education, music, drama, gymnastics and sport, dance, art, photography, ceramics, textiles, drawing, cookery and so on. But many schools choose to concentrate on one or a few specialist areas. Thus 10 of them are weighted towards the more physical disciplines of gymnastics and sport. Some specialise in music and theatre; others go for arts and crafts. There are schools that concentrate on the developing countries and schools that are orientated towards ecology and environmental protection. One school has film studies as its central subject.

For the sake of life

However, such a list gives very little idea of the special features of the Folk High Schools that have made them world-renowned as Denmark's contribution to international culture. One profound educational principle of the Folk High Schools is that the subjects taught are less important than the people who study them. In fact by law the schools must offer a "general education" and not compete with other sectors of the system or train pupils for specific jobs. Thus their primary purpose is to educate for life, to throw light on the fundamental questions of life as it is lived today, personally and socially. With no grade system, testing or examinations at the schools, the results achieved depend on the pupils' commitment and the teachers' ability to inspire.

The philosophy of the Folk High Schools springs from the Danish priest and cultural reformer N.F.S. Grundtvig, whose ideas are discussed elsewhere in this book (see index). All learning and human achievement, collective or individual, exists for the sake of life and not vice versa. The means should not be confused with the end. Pupils can acquire knowledge and learn skills, can stimulate their intellect and improve their technical prowess, but this in itself is of little help when faced with the fundamental questions that life asks of us.

Since noone has a solution to the riddle, the only way to approach an understanding is through talking together with people of different backgrounds and experiences. This "living conversation" is central to the Folk High Schools, which asks of its pupils not so much what they can do, but who are they and what do they believe in. Shared knowledge and applied skills are therefore an integral part of the process. Discovering oneself, relating to others, and conceiving a commitment to life are all part of the air one breathes at a Folk High School, imbuing it with an enthusiasm of spirit and a sense of community.

The social influence
of the Folk High School

The Folk High School tradition has played a considerable part in Danish political culture. When the schools came into being in the 1840s and 1850s the farmers who attended them in the winter months acquired a level of maturity and cultural awareness that enabled them to exploit the democratic rights laid down in the first Danish constitution of 1849. On that day in November 1844 the first Folk High School pupils to take their seats at a farm in Rødding, South Jutland, were 18 farmhands.

Over the next few years the classic form of the Folk High Schools began to emerge, thanks not least to Christen Kold (1816-1870), whose own teaching encapsulated the educational goals and methods of the Folk High School. His pupils were to be "enlivened" before they were "enlightened" – enthusiasm for a cause became its greatest motivator. Once when he was asked the purpose of his work, he pulled out his watch, began to wind it up and said, "I want to wind my pupils up, so that they never stop short." The art of his teaching was to call on the life in each child and help it to unfold; to achieve this, in place of the grind of rote learning, he told them stories, stories and more stories!

This oral, narrative culture, Grundtvig's "living word", proved to be of vital importance for the Folk High School movement. Often we can even see an opposition in principle to the written word, as when some schools forbade their pupils to take notes during a speaker's talk so as not to distract their own attention. For the speaker's words were designed to animate the subject for pupils rather than analyse it.

In 1864 Germany defeated Denmark in war and annexed the duchies of Schleswig and Holstein (some 40% of Denmark). The Danish response was summed up in the famous words of the politician Dalgas, "Replacement can be found for any loss we sustain, an outward loss must be turned to an inward gain." Within a decade 50 more Folk High Schools had sprung up throughout Denmark, guarding and developing the national spirit through the intensive study of Danish history, culture, language and nature. Only thus could the future be assured. And so paradoxically the defeat by Germany led to a blossoming of Danish culture and self-awareness. Closely linked to this was the farmers' development of a cooperative ideal which took the form of joint ownership of dairies and slaughterhouses, supply associations and stores, insurance companies and savings banks. The cooperative unions were borne along by a spirit of community manifested in the decision-making process of one man, one vote, whatever the size of business. There is a clear link here to the Folk High School tenet that each person is unique and incomparable.

The last 30 years of the 19th century were the classic period of Folk High Schools as they became a powerful cultural dynamic for the country, helping to produce the basis of the modern welfare state. In the course of the 20th century the labour movement has founded a number of its own Folk High Schools to give its members a sense of cultural history and self-respect. As the century has progressed, so has the range of new establishments, a more recent trend being towards the creative arts. This has been criticised by some as a form of escapism and defended by others as a retort to contemporary society instead of a replica of it. Indeed the ability of Folk High Schools to inspire alternatives to a utilitarian society, to be an experimental laboratory for self-awareness and enthusiastic committment, is a key reason for their existence – and for their success.

Free Schools

Grundtvig never set out a syllabus to be followed but kept his plans in general terms. This was not through lack of imagination but in order to prevent the Folk High School from being drawn up in a drawing-room. It is life at the school and what the pupils make of it that is the determining factor. Folk High Schools are "free schools" in the sense that each school creates its own curriculum and profile while maintaining the educative function required by law. Each in its own way is a radical alternative to the state education system.

Accordingly, foreign observers regularly comment on the paradox that the state gives considerable financial support to a school form that by law is forbidden to qualify its pupils for any sort of employment. This paradox is in fact the charm and the strength of the Folk High Schools. They exhibit a diversity of approach to a joint philosophy that neither the state nor any other public body should decide the right and only way to run a school or educate a person. Man, said Grundtvig, is a divine experiment.

On the other hand the freedom allowed, indeed encouraged, in the Folk High Schools is also characteristic of education legislation in general. By law Denmark has no compulsory schooling, only compulsory teaching. If a group of parents of a particular persuasion wish to set up a school for their children they have the right not only to do so but also to receive a state subsidy to help them run the school. Parents also have the right to educate their children at home instead of in school, provided there is a guarantee that the teaching actually takes place. Both people and parliament agree a monopoly of power is to be avoided at all costs.

This view of freedom has not come out of the blue. Its roots are to be found in the history of Denmark in the 19th century, where the popular will began to manifest itself against centralised state dictates. Ever since then it has been a national axiom that a freedom gained is a freedom defended.So the open exchange of ideas and experiences linked tothe community spirit of joint thought and action at a Folk High School provides a fertile soil in which freedom and the individual can thrive.

THE ROAD TO WISDOM

The road to wisdom? – Well, it's plain
and simple to express:
    Err
    and err
    and err again
    but less
    and less
    and less.

Piet Hein

9. Learning Teaching

Peder Kjøgx

We remember them from our own school-days – the good teachers. They combined their knowledge and personality with a presence that gave the lessons content and nerve. What did they have that made them unforgettable? Is it innate or acquired along the way or learned by flair and hard graft? And how do we begin to train such teachers professionally?

The professional teacher

Learning to teach is training for school reality. But what a teacher needs in order to make a lesson work and a school develop is the subject of considerable speculation and little agreement, professionally or politically. One thing that unites all Folkeskole teachers, however, is the awareness that the new Education Act of 1993 has placed new demands on them. Private practice behind the classoom door has once and for all been replaced by team-teaching; greater professional skills are required in subject teaching; and educational and psychological expertise is now taken for granted. In the professional debate teachers are expected to have the necessary skills to make decisions about planning and teaching and to be guaranteed conditions that allow them to develop relevant theory and practice in their locality. In short the reflecting teacher has replaced the reproducing teacher.

Teachers together, not just head teachers and senior staff, are now actively engaged in deciding on the school's focus, starting with the pupils and their future in society. The teachers' visions and experiences of systematic development are also acquiring similar importance in teacher training, resulting in a number of dilemmas in the colleges.

Educational practice and pluralism

At the training colleges there is no bell to divide up time in equal portions: a job is begun when it is important and ended when it is ready. There is a steady buzz around the place and an apparently unsystematic wandering around the well-equipped buildings by small groups in gymkit or wearing rubber boots and carrying fishing nets out of the building. The stink of hydrogen sulphide creeps out from under the door of a room while two young women walk past with a group of giggling children on their way to the library. A man is practising block letters on a blackboard with squeaky chalk that interrupts the animated discussion at the nearby table between students and teacher. Another cigarette is stubbed out, another cup of coffee is poured, another student is breast-feeding her baby.

Scenes from one of the 18 teacher training colleges around Denmark where the Education Act is being turned into action. They are run by a board of governors with local interests, but every decision is made in collaboration with staff and students. The teachers teach and guide, assess and evaluate, working within a syllabus framework laid down locally and planned in detail by staff and students alike. All examinations are public, most of them in the form of group exams in which students present a report to their teacher and a public examiner. Half the staff have a university background, the other half are themselves teacher-trained and have later taken a masters degree in Education through The Royal Academy for Pedagogical Studies, for the training colleges award teaching diplo-

mas only.

The multiplicity of educational practices and the everlasting debate on what constitutes good education often lead to passionate debate. What does one do in a particular classroom situation? Are certain practices more proper or more rewarding than others? How does one arrive at qualified decisions in a pluralist and democratic environment?

One key element in every debate is the conversation: the structured, professional conversation as well as the personal conversation that often involves existential questions. The starting-point of the conversation is vital: a definition of the situation, the aim, the qualifications and the roles. To listen and understand, to respect and learn, are as important as to talk and persuade. What is important is the benefit, the input is just the means. Can one truly learn anything one doesn't want to?

The group of giggling children and the two young women are back. They turn round and set off again, under the guidance of a girl filming with a video-camera. They are filming a scene for a media studies project – this is the fourth take.

Theory and practice

Surveys have shown that the actions of Folkeskole teachers in the classroom are motivated more by their own experiences as pupils than by their teacher training and classroom experience. Newly-trained teachers report a big difference between college knowledge and classroom practice, while the schools that welcome them are surprised to find that the colleges are being left behind by the pace of change. International surveys also suggest that Danish teachers lack the professional qualifications to put the Education Act into practice; comparisons with the other Nordic countries reveal a greater uncertainty in their subject among Danish teachers.

There is general agreement within the profession that the gap between theory and practice, college and classroom is still too wide. Moves are now being made to develop systematic reflection on planning, teaching and evaluating classroom practice to develop educational and subject skills both individually and in groups. Teaching practice during the 4-year college course is the obvious place to begin, with the keeping of diary notes, more personal guidance and improved supervision all playing a part in encouraging skills, confidence and self-reflection. Cooperation between college teachers, school teachers and college students is entering a new close-dialogue phase to help the student to teach the subject, understand the psychology, organise the classroom and become part of a teaching team.

The professional teacher and the private person

The backbone of a good school is the solid, independent teacher. As far back as 1789, during a crucial period of reform in Danish history, the absolute monarch King Frederik V took it upon himself to improve the quality of teaching in the Danish schools. Rather than rely on the universities he set up special colleges with contact to local life and schools, since when the debate has raged at local as well as national level as to what a teacher's role in society should be. Since parliamentary democracy was introduced in 1849, governments have worked hard and successfully to gain large majorities for Education Acts to ensure a certain continuity whatever the political colour of the government. At the same time debates on content and structure have often been of a more political and emotional nature than a sensible and analytical one.

So teachers have always been in the searchlight, open to assessment and criticism on every side, and since it cannot be otherwise, student teachers must be trained to deal with such situations and to

distinguish between their professional and private spheres by being aware of their choice of individual or team strategies. The current need for strong personalities who can meet the often conflicting demands of daily school life has increased the interest in who actually applies to become a teacher. Among successful applicants there is a wider demand for personal feedback and advice.

The average age of training college students is 22 at the beginning of their course, 60% of them being women. After leaving the Folkeskole at 16 most of them have a period of further study behind them, as well as a brief period with a private or public business. Most have been abroad for a time, and a number have attended a Folk High School; many men will have done their compulsory military service. In the cities, where the average age is higher, most students live in a relationship and many have had, or are having, their first child. Their choice of career is based on personal and professional experience, for which they have a sound basis on which to succeed and good eye for their future professional role.

Teachers also have the right to in-service training. Every year up to 25% of all teachers take part in a 1 to 3-day course, on application to their school, with the principal having the final say in where the limited financial resources are placed. 1-day courses often take place at the county Teaching Resource Centre, while 3-day courses with overnight stay are held at major course centres. The trend is towards school-based courses and training colleges are becoming increasingly involved. Participation is regarded as upgrading, though there is no pay increase involved.

Learning to teach is thus the first step on the road to a lifelong career, equipping teachers to face the future however the pupils, schools and society develop. Now they are teaching children to learn.

THAT IS THE QUESTION
Hamlet Anno Dominy.

Co-existence
or no existence.

Piet Hein

10. Lifelong Learning – Conditions and Trends

Peter Bacher

The need for lifelong learning has been pointed out time and again in recent years. The European Commission's white paper in 1993 and the report of the Industrial Research and Development Advisory Committee in 1994 (see Bibliography) emphasise that in a world characterised by increasing complexity and change the need to renew and update knowledge and skills is a lifelong concern. At a Nordic level a report was published early in 1995 by the Nordic Council of Ministers, the so-called Nordic Think Tank, entitled *The Golden Riches of Grass – Lifelong Learning for All*. This focuses on how the Nordic tradition and practice of popular education and adult teaching can inspire continued improvement in conditions for lifelong learning both in and outside the Nordic countries.

These and many other reports reflect the overriding agreement among researchers, politicians, leading business people and trade union representatives that the transition to a post-industrial society, the massive advances in technology, and the increasing internationalisation all lead in a single direction. In future people must possess a broad spectrum of qualifications in order to be able to manage at work, in society and in their private life.

Educating the whole person

The idea of "the whole person" and "the whole life" have become central to the debate, whether the starting-point is a streamlining of commercial life, the strengthening of democracy, the fight against unemployment or the lessening of social problems. Reflections on the qualifications and skills needed for the future revolve around people being active individuals. In addition to possessing in-depth skilled knowledge and insight they must be able to evaluate and communicate, be flexible and mobile, step in and out of social networks and participate in decision-making. They must also be creative enough for their acquired skills and knowledge to be combined and utilised in new ways. It is repeatedly stressed that the most important qualification is the ability to learn afresh – right through life. This involves the ability not only "to learn to learn" but also to set aside obsolete knowledge that prevents new knowledge from being acquired.

Such matters have been discussed for years by those involved in the adult education sector: researchers, teachers, experts and representatives from the organisations. But with the drastic changes in work patterns in recent years the issues have spread to a much wider circle, and adult education is now a major point on the national agenda. Concepts such as "lifelong learning" and "recurrent education" have acquired a new and wider significance since supplementary training, updating qualifications and skills development have become central themes in the labour market debate.

The debate is also linked to the concept of democracy, which involves not only political awareness but also self-awareness. To this end education must also serve. As *Adult Education and the Concept of Popular Education* (1993) made clear:

"It is of importance to emphasize the relation between democracy and popular education. In his book *What is democracy?* from 1945 the Danish theologian Hal Koch underlines what is still relevant today:" ...democracy can never be guaranteed. It is not a system which has to be established but a lifestyle that is not be adopted. It is a question of sentiment which must be conveyed through generations; that is why "popular education" is the core of democracy."

Such questions are currently being debated in Denmark under the headlines: Qualifications for the Future, Skills 2000, Learning Organisations, Developing Work and Human Resources at Work. Popular education and its role in lifelong learning are also under discussion. Although Denmark has a long tradition of general adult education – the "general" being an important element in the coming years – a question mark is being placed on the value of a number of courses currently being offered. Thus limits have been set on the access of unemployed people to the Folk High Schools and the new Day High Schools.

The tradition of popular education mentioned in the opening chapter and elsewhere deserves further discussion since it is a distinguishing feature of the Danish scene and a viable alternative that has already been successfully exported. The following is therefore an outline of the institutional framework and conditions for lifelong learning in Denmark today, with the focus on adult education, on where Denmark differs from other countries and on the latest reforms and developments.

Popular education – available choices

The Danish tradition of popular education, with the Folk High School as the best-known example, has been marketed so effectively abroad that many visitors to Denmark expect to find one in every village and large numbers of Danes attending regularly throughout their lives.

However, the reality at the turn of the millennium is that there are no more than 100 schools, accommodating 60,000 students or 1 in 85 of the Danish population per year, with the vast majority attending 1 or 2-week courses only. Around 12,000 take part in the longer courses (4-6 months), most of them young people. Four out of five on courses lasting over 5 weeks are under 25 years old. Many have a Gymnasium education behind them and regard 6 months at a Folk High School as a rounding-off of their academic education with something more creative and less stressful.

The Folk High Schools look at the world around us, encourage us to reflect, allow us to concentrate on a particular interest, and offer discussion on equal terms on life's big questions. All without examinations. They are a breath of fresh air for all who attend, but particularly for the 1 in 10 youngsters who come for 6 months to re-charge their batteries and make future plans after 9 to 13 years in school – the final years under considerable pressure. Alongside the Folk High Schools other types of education have grown up which in quantity actually occupy a much larger position for youngsters and adults.

The Folk High Schools belong to the circle of educational institutions that are designated "free schools", i.e. state-subsidised independent schools offering courses of their own form and content. In Denmark there are 9 years of compulsory teaching by law, but there is no compulsory schooling. In other words parents can teach their children at home. Or they can set up private schools with an 85% state subsidy for the teaching budget. Roughly 10% of Danish children attend such schools. They may be free schools with a particular religious, educational or political slant, such as Muslim schools or Rudolf Steiner schools or just small-scale alternatives to the state schools. All of

them, however, must live up to the general framework laid down by the Education Act.

The Continuation Schools are boarding schools for 14 to 18-year-olds that follow the Folkeskole curriculum. Around 13% of young people spend their last two years here, often those who need to leave home and school for one reason or another. Again there is an 85% state subsidy for the teaching budget, with local councils usually providing pupil grants. Other free schools include Domestic Schools and Craft Schools. Agricultural Schools also used to belong in this category, but 10 years ago their administration was transferred to the vocational schools, since they were primarily qualifying schools for further studies.

Adult education outside school

Associations and societies, including a huge range of sports clubs, are also part of the general adult education picture in Denmark, which is often called "the land of societies". A few statistics illustrate this. There are 17,000 societies receiving local council support. The Danish Youth Council (DUF) is an umbrella organisation for some 50 youth organisations with around 1 million members. The two biggest sports organisations each have about 1½ million members in their local organisations. Organisations for the elderly have over 700,000 members, involving 70% of the over-60s.

Evening Schools and Day High Schools are also part of the general education scene. The Evening Schools, which run relatively short courses amounting to between 20-40 lessons, are increasingly being run during the daytime. There are well over a million participants (1 in 5 of all Danes) every year and a wide range of courses is on offer, including foreign languages, computer studies, creative arts, physical training, cultural talks and so on. The Day High Schools, which offer whole-day teaching for a period of a few months, appeal especially to the unemployed and social security recipients.

A number of school forms which historically have developed as evening classes and education associations are still decentralised in form. They belong within the adult education teaching tradition and are county financed. These include Special Needs teaching and Immigrant teaching as well as the formal Adult Education Centres (VUC) which qualify for examinations at the same level as the Folkeskole's leaving examination. Local council Youth Schools also have their origins in popular education. In their leisure-time over half of all 14 to 18-year-olds today frequent these schools, which offer teaching in general subjects such as cooking, first aid and photography as well as a vigorous club activity. Production Schools for 18 to 25-year-olds offer practical and theoretical teaching particularly to unemployed young people. The priority here is teaching work skills. Though not providing any formal qualifications they build confidence for further education and/or job searching.

A third main area of popular education is provided by the cultural institutions of Denmark, which have traditionally had a popular strain. Some museums, galleries, libraries and theatres like to regard themselves as popular educators (in the sense that they help to educate the people), but it would be fairer to say that they are educational rather through their audience, visitors or book-borrowers being active in a collective social context. In this broader definition, for example, activities linked to the local historical archives, to amateur theatre, to illustrated talks followed by discussion at the local library, or to study groups at the art museum can be regarded as popular education. However, the border between this and a more individual approach to culture is somewhat vague.

Last but by no means least we find adult

education outside the institutions, that is, activities taking place in the local parish hall or church hall, cultural centre, commune, school, nursery or the like, where people get together often across the generations for activities that can range from meal-sharing to specific purposes such as running a cinema where there is no commercial basis for it or building a children's playground in the local village.

The limits of adult and popular education

The above presentation reveals that popular education covers a whole range of activities that cannot be delimited by age, content or form. Its characteristic features are described thus in *The Golden Riches in the Grass*:

"At its very core popular education is a counter-culture. It arose as a protest against the dominance of the few over the many. One of its key features is *voluntarism*. The sole prior requirement for participation is the desire to participate. And the yield? That must be assessed by the participants themselves. In this context, curriculum requirements, tests and examination certificates are usually extraneous elements. Another characteristic is *free initiative*. This applies to the right to implement an idea, to the choice of subject and choice of teacher. In popular education all are of equal merit, though they may not be equally knowledgeable. The basic assumption is that the individual human being is a valuable experiment, and can develop his or her potential only when freedom prevails. A third characteristic is the spirit of *liberalism*. The popular education movement acknowledges that the different ideas and attitudes found among people must have an equal right to a platform. Each person must reach his or her own interpretation of the meaning of life and at the same time allow other people's interpretations to be considered. The right of other people to maintain their viewpoints must be respected, even though one need not respect the actual points of view"
.

It is a feature of popular education that there is an open debate as to its limits. Certain Folk High Schools consider the activities of their nearest neighbour as not "right and proper" for a Folk High School; the teachers may even be "heretics"! In other clubs and associations or educational institutions with a hierarchical structure, where the teaching largely consists of one-way communication, the words "popular education" are like a watchword which opens up the public moneybox even though it is a far cry from a conversation between equal partners.

Evaluation and delimitation of what popular education constitutes is for the most part left to the individual, free schools and committees to be found in every one of the country's 275 municipalities. The local council committees for popular education distribute funding to the clubs and societies and to Evening School teaching as well as ensuring that by law at least 5% of the combined funding is used on "new initiatives, development research, places where popular education is the main purpose, as well as to activities of a cross-subject nature".

It is important to note that there is no Act of Parliament governing adult education, only an Act "supporting popular education". For it is impossible to legislate for what popular education is; instead grants are made to institutions or activities where popular education *may* take place.

Popular education circles often discuss the limits of their branch. There is antipathy to highbrow culture, which is seen as the antithesis of popular culture, a kind of snob culture. Another border has to do with the "social" element. Even though there is a markedly social dimension to

the concept of popular education – the actual togetherness of it – there is often widespread scepticism about the enveloping and debilitating effects that welfare culture can have on the case worker/client relationship. A third border is the one verging on the criminal. The law allows, for example, biker groups such as Hell's Angels to become associations and receive a grant for the upkeep of their premises, no matter how many members may be in prison for criminal offences. Since the "biker wars" on the streets of Denmark in 1995-96, however, the law has been tightened so that demonstrably criminal groups are no longer eligible for a grant.

Another case involving the Folk High Schools gained press coverage in summer 1995 under the headline "Golf War". It transpired that certain schools were offering 1-week courses in golf, tennis and surfing. Legislation on this point is clear: at least one-third of the teaching must be general and shared (study groups, class teaching, conversation groups, talks etc.) The courses were withdrawn. A further episode that featured in the national press was the "Camel Riding Case" when unemployed people on a 3-month Day High School course about the Danish attitude to foreign cultures were sent on a 2-week trip to Tunisia on very favourable terms.

Such current examples, though completely uncharacteristic, nevertheless show that legislation on popular education does have limits, however broad, and rests on the mutual trust that at local levels funds will be used in accordance with the purpose for which they were designated. Added to this is the general acceptance that those who take initiatives in popular education activities must show tact and discretion so as not to outrage public feeling, for example by advertising their courses in such a way that they rightly or wrongly are regarded as good holiday offers or individual pleasure pursuits.

Other adult education opportunities

Adult education in Denmark also includes courses for unskilled and upgraded workers (AMU courses) usually full-time from 1 to 15 weeks. In addition AMU centres offer in-service training for skilled workers and supervisors.

Commercial and Technical Schools are also increasing their activities in adult education, typically in single-subject courses. By contrast, the universities play a much lesser role, the one important exception being the University Extension Courses, which under the same law for the Evening Schools offer all manner of courses and lectures. Perhaps as a result of the powerful tradition for adult education the idea of an Open University arrived late on the scene in Denmark, where it is limited primarily to teachers in adult education.

Finally there are a number of county education institutions and projects that take care partly of in-service training for their personnel and partly of the educational needs of the unemployed. Businesses provide their own training schemes or call in private educational firms, but they also make considerable use of the public education system, including the vocational schools and the AMU centres for upgrading.

Participant profiles

There is a predominance of women participants on the general adult education courses, while the vocational courses are attended primarily by men. The trend in the last decade is towards an equalisation of the sexes. This is particularly true of the many experiments, grant-aided developmental courses programmes where "cross-sector" courses are available which combine general and vocational teaching.

As regards social class it is no surprise that the AMU courses for unskilled and upgraded workers recruit people with the minimum education. The same goes for the VUCs, the formal Adult Education Centres. Evening Schools appeal to a broad range of the population but differ markedly from other courses by having a relatively high age quotient.

Opening the system
- increased flexibility

The 1994 Act on open education provided three major opportunities:
1) All full-time youth and adult education can be taken part-time 2) All previous part-time education can be taken as full-time 3) Teaching can take place both in the daytime and the evening. Under certain conditions those who provide private courses can also receive state subsidies.

At the same time a new labour market reform came into force which included provisions for leave or time-off for education upgrading, child-minding or a sabbatical. The reform also increased the opportunity to create courses that would help the unemployed back into work. Leave of absence from the labour market in order to upgrade one's education had already been available for employed adults with a minimum education via an adult education grant (VUS); the new provision now allowed leave to practically anyone with unemployment insurance whether they were employed or not.

Financial support for adults upgrading under these provisions corresponds to the top maintenance allowance. This is relatively high in Denmark, approaching the minimum wage for unskilled workers. Since public and private employers have by and large topped up the grant to the full wage the provision has met with huge success. Courses are often organised on a job rotation basis, i.e. a group of unemployed people often deputize for staff who are on leave. The former are thus in work for a period during which they can try to establish themselves on the labour mar-

ket, while the latter are improving their education and job skills; finally the state saves on maintenance allowances and the unemployment rate drops.

Coupled with previous provisions for the long-term unemployed which included compulsory educational training these new reforms have highlighted the need for the various adult education institutions to cooperate to a much higher degree on planning courses, running cross-sector courses (general and voactional), and providing information and guidance in the process. Participants have often left school at 16 and had little or no further training, which means that courses for them need to be tailor-made.

Other innovations in recent years include vocational basic training (EGU), individually organised youth training (FUU) and the bridgebuilding course linking the Folkeskole to the vocational courses of the Commercial and Technical Schools or to the more academic courses of the Gymnasium and HF. All three build on the principle of bringing together elements from various courses already in existence and require a fair degree of cooperation between the institutions involved as well as a comprehensive information and guidance programme. Another recent advance in adult education was the establishment in 1996 of free courses for those who feel their reading, writing and spelling abilities are poor, an offer which follows the lines of courses already available to dyslexics.

Lastly the Ministry of Education is working on a merit system that will enable youngsters and adults to move between the various Gymnasium/HF and Commercial/Technical courses in future.

The 10-point plan ten years on

The last ten years have been marked by a series of development programmes that in various ways, directly and indirectly, have increased the opportunities for adults to get into more or less formal learning processes. The 10-point programme for adult and popular education in 1984 led to a whole range of experiments, the results of which were included in the revised Leisure-time Education Act and in the curriculum and examination forms of basic adult education. This was followed by the 7-point programme for the Folkeskole as a local cultural centre (see p.109). Next came the programme for social development resources and the cultural ideas programme, which aimed among other things to promote collaboration between amateurs and professionals.

In 1995 the Ministry of Education produced a second 10-point plan on recurrent education to build on the first:

1. Everyone shall be given the opportunity for a grant for adult education. Special rights are allowed for those who had only a minimum education in their younger years.

2. More educational institutions shall offer and organise adult education.

3. In the Folkeskolen and in secondary education (16 to 19) the basic concept of recurrent education shall be inculcated.

4. The educational institutions shall be committed to updating participants' education and give a "recharge" guarantee.

5. Greater cohesion and transparency shall be ensured via an extensive merit system and wider access for the individual on his/her own responsibility.

6. Adult education institutions and businesses shall be urged to open up to each other with a view to entering into a mutually binding collaboration.

7. Cross-sector cooperation between educational insitutions offering vocational, general and popular education shall be expanded so that each contributes with its own particular strengths.

8. New information technology in adult education shall give access to acquiring new knowledge from the whole world and creating greater flexibility in the organisation of all education courses.

9. An electronic data processing catalogue shall be built up covering the entire range of adult educational opportunities.

10. Adult education shall be developed via the Internet, where the opportunities are many and where a dynamic network offers the individual access according to need and motivation.

The plan was launched in the middle of a lengthy discussion on the content, organisation and financing of the future adult education system. "The adult and in-service training reform", as it was called, was then debated by the four involved parties: the state, including the government; the local councils and county councils; the employers' organisations; and the employees' organisations. Among the subjects under discussion were:

1) How comprehensive should in-service training be, and with what aim – labour-related, educational or social?

2) Who should finance which courses – the tax-payers, participants, businesses or others demanding qualifications?

3) To what degree should the supply and demand side of adult education be regulated?

4) How should collaboration between institutions be encouraged when decentralisation and cash-per-student grants are creating potential competition?

Learning by other means

While there is a general consensus that the effort to improve qualifications and skills throughout the population is absolutely essential, there is still widespread disagreement as to how to organise and finance it. Lifelong learning has become a magic formula for politicians as well as a mantra for decision-makers. The lack of concrete initiatives to implement the plans is due to the various underlying interpretations of what adult education, popular education and lifelong learning actually involve. It is everything from a necessary evil to a bid for higher productivity and profit to a lifeform that ensures that all members of society are politically aware, resourceful and democratically resolved.

Matters have not been made easier by the traditionally reactionary attitude of the education services towards adult education. As Søren Dupont points out in *Qualifications and Popular Education* (1995):

"Throughout history the problem for the education sector has been that every time society and business requires the individual to learn new skills, the educational institutions respond with a repetition of a medieval teaching process, as if nothing had happened in between. In the current situation this is impossible. The educational tools of "copy, repeat, correct" remain active and dominant learning principles...we are at the end of an epoch with the birth of a new indivisible unity of qualifications that cannot be separated into work, private life and social life. The dissolution of the medieval crafts makes learning by other means absolutely essential."

The development of teaching forms and methods such as open and distance learning (ODL) in various technologically-aided areas, individualised learning, project and problem-centred education, dual training (sandwich courses), peer learning, etc. are obvious possibilities. Alongside them comes the major challenge to answer the basic question: why do we learn at all and how do we create the optimal conditions for doing so?

Apparently not everyone learns in the same way. For some people learning situations are quite pleasurable, for others the opposite. Some are quick to grasp a particular type of knowledge by reading about it, while others learn better through oral communication, social togetherness, practical work, model teaching and so on. Some are especially motivated to learn if there is a practical purpose in view, others think that theoretical knowledge is a goal in itself. Some find it hard to transfer knowledge and experience from one situation to another, others find it easy. Why is this so, we ask. How does one learn to be creative, is it indeed possible? Who learns best under which circumstances, formal or informal?

Surprisingly little is known about these areas. We know on the other hand a lot about our "social inheritance" and our desire to learn, or lack of it, in particular social groups. We are beginning to learn something about how particular types of people can acquire the desire to learn through introductory courses, often of some length, that give them self-confidence and a general zest for life. We also know that we can successfully employ "medieval" teaching forms if we wish to achieve measurable results in our learners. But it can all certainly be done much better, and the coming years should see a closer examination of such questions through large-scale research, experiment and development.

The most important political task for

adult education is to create a framework that maximises opportunities for unorganised learning. Those who take a year off not only report deep satisfaction; the personal boost they have had can also be seen on their faces. It affects their workplace, their friends, their whole social life. A year off work for reconsideration and self-development on a full wage and without any control should be a human right.

FREEDOM

Freedom means
you're free to do
just whatever
pleases you;
- if, of course
that is to say,
what you please
is what you may.

Piet Hein

11. Educational Change
– Forums for Debate and Decision

Johannes Nymark

The basis of the Danish educational system is the Folkeskole. Since it is mixed-sex and fully-comprehensive from ages 6 to 16 it naturally arouses great interest. Throughout the country its content and future are the subject of lively debate, coloured by personal philosophies and political leanings and closely linked to the whole sensitive question of child-rearing. Hardly has society registered a new problem before the school is requested to take care of it. Few local decisions can create such ardour and ire as political decisions to open or close schools, rebuild or re-equip them, change their structure or content.

More recently this concern has been extended to include education for the 16 to 19-year-olds, doubtless because the vast majority of youngsters leaving the Folkeskole now opt for further education. Only 30 years ago the Gymnasium (upper secondary school) was the prerogative of the most gifted 10% of a year. The rest acquired apprenticeships, supplemented with limited theoretical training in the Commercial and Technical Schools, or went straight into full-time paid work, earning their first wages at the age of 17.

Historically, however, there is a big difference between the Gymnasium and the various other forms of education available to school-leavers, even though formally they are controlled by the same parliament, as the following will demonstrate.

The Folkeskole

The Danish Folkeskole is well on the way to celebrating its bicentenary. Its second century has had a long tradition of experiment and reform. Nowadays politicians,

school leaders, staff and occasionally parents, pupils and newspapers are all motivators of new thinking. In fact in the last 30 years or so one school reform has hardly been agreed upon before another is being talked about. Reforms thus often start from below. Such was the case in the wake of the 1975 Education Act, at a time when women were joining the labour force in ever-increasing numbers. In the last decade single-parent families have also changed the face of education.

As a result teachers have gradually adopted some of the attitudes and burdens of social workers, and child-rearing has begun to compete with traditional teaching as the schools' prime concern. Under the pressure of performing these conflicting roles the Danish Union of Teachers, a powerful and relatively united body, put pressure on Parliament in 1987 to pass a 7-point programme of renewal which included turning schools into cultural as well as educational centres. The tradition of change from below was even integrated into the system as parliament gave schools a major grant for experimental education over a 4-year period. Some of this money was used for an evaluation of current experiments with a view to passing a new act of parliament.

A commission was set up that demonstrates the breadth of interest in the Folkeskole; it contained education experts and representatives from among parents, pupils, school leaders, education directors, county and municipal councils, the National Sports Council, the Council for Adult Education, the Danish Youth Council, and the Independent Schools Council.

Over 7,000 experiments large and small

were carried out at schools throughout the country. Reports of these, successful or otherwise, were summarised and given to politicians, there were debates throughout the system, and based in this way on inspiration from below the new Education Act became law in 1993. A new framework rather than a new content was the result, requiring increased in-service training for teachers, whose workload now included occasional 1-subject-only schooldays, seminars, special projects and so on.

Recurrent training

Extra grants were made available for the purpose-oriented courses run by training colleges, county and municipal education centres, and not least by the Royal Danish School of Educational Studies (DLH). DLH is the flagship of in-service training and the main evaluator of the above-mentioned experiments. With its comprehensive state-funded programme of semester and year-courses nationwide it keeps teachers abreast of the latest educational theories and practices in every imaginable area. Course participants are given time off school to attend (paid for by local councils), typically for one afternoon a week.

The country's 18 Teacher Training colleges also offer in-service courses, and many of their staff are involved in research projects at selected schools. However, the increase in the number of courses available has not been matched by local council willingness to fund their side of the agreement, with the result that disappointment has spread among teachers who are being asked to implement new practices, such as in computing, that they are not yet trained for.

Political awareness that the Folkeskole must continue to renew itself has been recognised in the Act through the establishment of a Folkeskole Council, which shall "advise the Minister of Education in all questions concerning the folkeskole including proposals for research and development." For this purpose among others local councils employ hundreds of educational consultants in specific subject areas, but the variation in political priorities in the country's 275 local councils means that available resources for the local Folkeskoler are far from uniform.

The Gymnasium and HF

Superficially there are a number of similarities between the Folkeskole (from 6-16) and the subsequent 3-year Gymnasium and 2-year Higher Preparatory Course (HF), for example in the subjects on offer and the daily routine. On average pupils sit in classes of 24 from 08.00 to 14.00 or 15.00, with periods of 45 minutes followed by 5 or 10-minute breaks with ½ hour for lunch. They may have up to 7 different subjects a day, but the average is 4-5.

Historically and politically, however, the Folkeskole and the Gymnasium differ widely. The Folkeskole is run locally and its teachers are purpose-trained at colleges; the Gymnasium is run centrally and its teachers are university-trained in one or two subjects. University courses give access to a wide range of jobs, one of which may be teaching, but not until they have left university (after 6 years and with two subjects) do graduates who want to teach begin the task of mediating their knowledge to 16 to 19-year-olds. In fact they are appointed to Gymnasium posts on the quality of their university results before they actually begin training. This takes place at another school under the guidance of three or four experienced teachers. Thus for their first year out of university they are teaching at one school, training at another and attending in-service courses on the theory of education and the two subjects they are now teaching, an impressive workload indeed.

The transition from the Folkeskole to the

Gymnasium at 16 can seem equally demanding for pupils, especially since the Gymnasium immediately treats them as free but responsible young adults and begins to loosen the strong parent-pupil-teacher links of the Folkeskole.

The Gymnasium and HF are financed by the county councils but administered centrally by a directorate immediately under the Minister of Education. Thus there is limited local political interest in them and with far fewer interested parties the educational debate at this level is carried on largely by members of parliament and school principals and staff, with pupils joining in now and again with limited success.

Over the past 25 years the formal structure of the Gymnasium and HF has seen relatively few changes, but educational content and methodology have undergone radical development as the pupil intake has increased from 10% to 40% of a year. When the pupils' desire for influence began to meet the teachers' demand for in-depth learning an interesting form of democracy appeared in the classroom – a dialogue that forced pupils to acknowledge their personal responsibility and teachers to re-think their educational practices. Another remarkable feature at this level is that within certain relatively free limits laid down centrally, teacher and class can decide on their own course of studies.

The decentralised structure, the lack of formality, and the high power and quality of the teachers' professional associations are all major factors in developing the Gymnasium and HF. The teachers' considerable influence on their two subjects feeds back into the system in the form of teaching commitment, and this above all has enabled them to make the transition from teaching an elite to teaching a broad range of youngsters.

Vocational training
– the Commercial and Technical Schools

Denmark has a long tradition of training for handicrafts and other vocations. On leaving school apprentices would train under master builders, shop owners, factory managers and so on, and after 3-4 years acquire their journeyman's certificate under an external examiner. First in their leisure-time, later as part of their working day, this training was supplemented by studies at Commercial or Technical School. In line with the increasing demand for skilled qualifications – not least as a result of increased industrialisation and a wider use of technology – the system was criticised, particularly by the iron and steel and engineering industries. As a result a full-time basic vocational training (EFG) course was introduced. This time it was industry pressing for renewal.

The course consisted of a year's general studies at school and a broad introduction to the various skilled trades followed by two years of more specific training alternating between school and a workplace. The experiment proved to be so successful that it was turned into an Act of Parliament in the late 1970s. Since there was also a majority for retaining the old master/apprentice courses in certain fields the two continued side by side for some years, but the competition as to their relative merits became so intolerable that in 1989 a further reform was introduced, more in the spirit of what was politically feasible than as a result of acquired experience. Some of the positive innovations, particularly in the basic year, were lost in the reform.

As can be seen vocational training has had a rather chequered career over the past 20 years. Rapid and wide-ranging reforms have caused painful readjustments in the vocational schools and in contrast to their colleagues in the Gymna-

sium and HF vocational teachers have had little or no influence on this development, which has been controlled by a large network of councils and committees on which employer and employee representatives have had a dominant influence. This influence also stretches deep into the corridors of Parliament.

Thus educational policy for the vocational schools is organised to suit the needs of the existing labour market and is controlled by the ongoing requirements of employers and unions. They it is who formulate demands for renewal, primarily through the Danish Employers' Association (DA) and the Danish Federation of Trade Unions (LO), while Government ministers and Members of Parliament draw up the necessary legislation.

These many and various changes have required much in-service retraining for teachers to implement them, a task not made easier by the very diverse backgrounds from which they came into teaching. A new institution, the State Institute for the Educational Training of Vocational Teachers (SEL) was therefore established to define and meet their needs, playing much the same role for vocational schoolteachers as DLH does for Folkeskole teachers (see above). SEL's purpose-oriented efforts have given a much-needed lift to teachers and their qualifications, but even more important for renewal in vocational training will be SEL's research programme, which will focus on educational theory and practice in vocational training independent of the powerful interests of the competing parties involved in the labour market. For as the pressure for ever-new technology grows, so does the welter of demands on the vocational schools, and the need for independent thought, research and reflection is now central to the their success. Perhaps through SEL teachers too can make their voices heard.

Lastly, in the competition with the Gym-

nasium and HF for school-leavers from the Folkeskole the recruitment of teachers with a wide range of backgrounds and new qualifications is in itself a way of renewing educational practice in the Commercial and Technical Schools.

Summary

Most young people complete 12-13 years of school before they move on to the labour market or to further education. It is logical that the various forms of schooling should therefore be thought of as variations on a single theme, but this unfortunately is not the case. Not through lack of desire but because structures and administrative conditions more or less prevent it – both internally and externally. On one point, however, there has been a common development throughout the educational system: the individual institutions have acquired more self-determination and all now have a school board of governors of some kind or another.

In the Folkeskole the school board is dominated by parent representatives and has some power, whereas in the Gymnasium it is more representative – with staff, pupils, parents, local business people and a local politician – but has only relatively modest influence. Local business people predominate on the vocational school boards.

There is therefore at present no natural link between the three main areas that educate the youth of Denmark. However, there is a powerful movement gaining ground to build bridges between the Folkeskole and the other two. Counsellors, and in particular local council youth counsellors who follow youngsters through the years immediately after leaving the Folkeskole at the age of 16, have pointed to the absolute necessity of further training before any attempt is made to join the labour market, such are the demands for skilled workers nowadays.

Unfortunately many young people find

the transition difficult from the Folkeskole to the Gymnasium/HF or the Commercial/Technical School. Traditionally there has been no continuity from the one to the others, either vertically or horizontally. This may explain why it is only now that the transition is becoming a political problem. And again it is the school guidance counsellors, the teachers and the school principals who register the problem. Since the 10th school year, at the end of the Folkeskole, has traditionally been an optional year, it is now being experimented with as a bridge year to further training in the Gymnasium/HF or the Commercial/Technical School. Teachers from all the school forms are working together to bridge the gap by providing "taster" courses with elements from both school forms and by experimenting with all manner of educational methods and practices.

Provisional results are encouraging. More youngsters are staying on to complete 13 years of education and teachers are getting to know each other's school systems and best of all educational methods. So these transitional classes are becoming a platform for a very useful job-training for the teachers involved. Optimistically this collaboration will create new ideas and practices between the older classes of the Folkeskole and the courses in the vocational schools – again an innovation from below.

Education – a national interest

Every Danish educational form has undergone change and reform in recent years. The innovations will continue for some time to come as in-service training, school development, and experimental work take hold. Until, that is, the need is felt from below for a more formal change in the system, and the politicians step in to create a framework and lay down goals. For change from below is fundamental to Danish education. Pupils, teachers, parents, heads and principals are at the centre of the constantly changing daily reality, reacting to new problems and challenges, testing solutions, and bringing about innovation in small steps.

Crucial to the quality of educational policy in Denmark therefore is the politicians' respect for change from below. Of course they too have goals and can envisage the means to achieve them, but both goals and means must be pursued in harmony with the will for change that arises in the individual schools.

THE WISDOM OF THE SPHERES

How instructive
is a star !
It can teach us
from afar
just how small
each other are.

Piet Hein

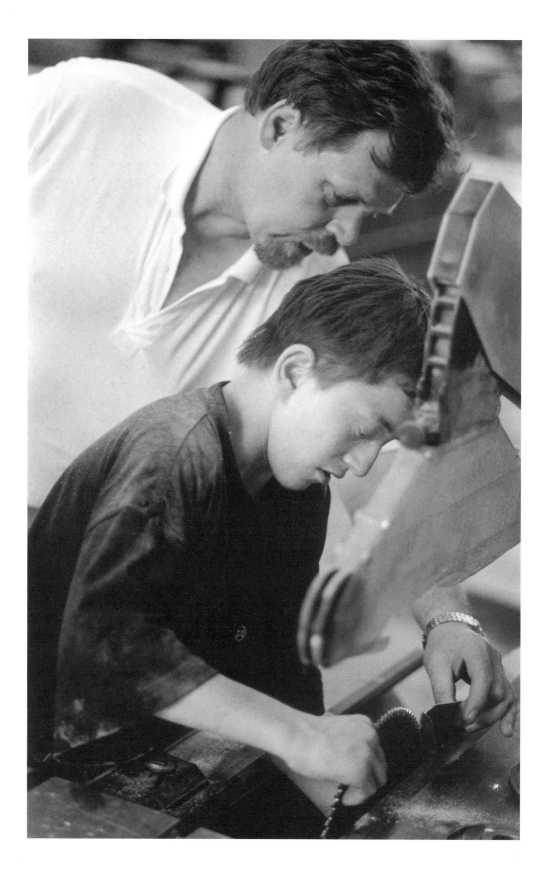

12. Quality and Quantity – Creating, Running and Evaluating Educational Institutions

Olav Harsløf

The Danish contribution to the American defeat of Iraq in the Gulf War in 1991 was a hospital ship manned by Danish doctors and other personnel. This excellent example of Danish technology and know-how all rolled into one had hardly arrived in the Gulf, however, before it was made abundantly clear by the Americans that none of their troops under any circumstances would place themselves under the knives of Danish surgeons. If the ship and the hospital staff were to serve any purpose, it would have to be the wounded and captured Iraqis who placed themselves in Danish hands.

The snub aroused consternation in Denmark, where Danish doctors are widely considered to be among the world's best, their training second to none in Europe. Danish doctors indeed have never found reason to make a positive comparison with the American health service, frowning upon the conspicuous class divisions of its patients and the general quality of public health service available.

Myths and reality

In fact Danes have long believed that their school system, their vocational training and their levels of science are at the top of the scale on a global measurement. And with some justification. For from the turn of the century until the late 1960s Danish teachers, with their broad professional training, were internationally regarded as being among the leaders in their field. The same was true of Danish scientists and scholars, with such figures as the cultural critic Georg Brandes (1842-1927), the dermatologist Niels Finsen (1860-1904), the bacteriologist Carl Julius Salomonsen

(1847-1924), the physicist Niels Bohr (1885-1962), the linguist Louis Hjelmslev (1899-1965) and the music theorist Knud Jeppesen (1892-1974). People such as these had made Denmark famous throughout the universities of the world. A Danish doctorate, in its demands for scientific rigour, is not exceeded anywhere in the world and is vastly superior to, for example, a Swedish or a German one.

Thus, when 12 principals of private Gymnasia in Denmark on a study-trip to English schools, colleges and universities in the mid-1980s were invited to lunch with their English counterparts by a Cambridge dean, they soon discovered that they had considerably higher qualifications than their English colleagues. A Danish principal might have 6-8 years study of Mathematics, Physics and Chemistry, while his English colleague had 4 years in one subject. Another Dane could have an MA and a Ph D. in Danish Literature, or have studied two major subjects such as English and History for 6-8 years. The English colleague would turn out to have a 4-year MA in English (specialising in Elizabethan literature) or History (specialising in Byzantine history). Unsolicited the English declared that their university education was too short and too narrow. They kept referring to the endless cuts in the British education system, and did not feel that their Danish colleagues could acquire much wisdom or many educational ideas from Cambridge. By and large they were right.

And yet English scholarship manages very well. Despite a down-at-heel state education system and an almost impene-

trable maze of private schools and further education courses England also turns out plenty of clever teachers, academics, technicians and researchers.

To focus on quality

The quality of a given course of training is relatively difficult to measure and can barely be seen with the naked eye. Whether one walks around a new Commercial School in England with superb teaching facilities, libraries, an audio-visual department, a large canteen, an assembly hall, a huge foyer with a fountain and good facilities for teachers, or around a private boarding school in the country that looks like a manor-house, with a pleasant dayroom and classrooms, large playing-fields and capacious gymnasia one gets the feeling of unmistakable quality. By way of contrast a look-in on schools and institutes housed in former residential properties, factory shops or plain old huts reveals the other side of the fence.

But whatever a school's physical reality, its reputation is always largely based on what can briefly be termed internal professional and social communication. Are the children learning? Are they happy? In Copenhagen, where pupils can freely choose among 20 different Gymnasia, the oldest and most dilapidated colleges, next to noisy stations or in areas infiltrated with drugs and prostitution, are among the most popular.

There is much to suggest that quality should be measured in terms of "previous record" rather than from analyses of what is happening here and now. And the most measurable factor available is the promotion of successful candidates to higher things or the recognition that the majority of the school's pupils have "done well for themselves". Once an institution has acquired a reputation for providing good futures, its reputation is assured for a good while to come. This is another reason why Niels Bohr still means so much to the international reputation of Danish physics several decades after his death. The same goes for linguistic research in the light of Louis Hjelmslev.

On a lower level a good head teacher or classroom teacher is the measure of quality. It is rarely the curriculum or the amount of work that is the criterion. Yet human qualities are in fact rarely mentioned until they are missed further up the scale – often many years afterwards.

Formal and informal qualifications

It is maintained that very few Danes are qualified for European Union appointments in the bureaucracy. They are poorly equipped not only linguistically but also professionally. The blame is placed first on the shoulders of the basic school, the Folkeskole, for a lack of written ability; then on the Gymnasium for poor linguistic ability; and finally on the universities for uncertainty and poor judgement. However, Danes know that they speak good English, German and French, and that private firms and public administration are perfectly satisfied with the skills of their staff. Applicants for European Union appointments fall down on their "Danish behaviour": their corduroy trousers and cowboy jeans, their sandals and sweatshirts, their joviality and their cups of coffee. This is not how it is done in the land of jackets and ties and long dresses and a genderless linguaphone language. On the other hand it would appear that when it comes to working elsewhere abroad the Danish education system, with its greater emphasis on social insight and creative initiative rather than legal poise and eloquence, is a far better qualifier for the less tailor-made, more challenging jobs in the developing countries or other areas undergoing political and economic change, such as Eastern Europe. Too much *Yes Minister* and similar TV series have made it difficult for Danes to take the Brussels lifestyle seriously.

In depth and in breadth

Nonetheless there must be a reason why American soldiers at war question the Danish education system, in this case the training of doctors. The reason is in fact general knowledge among Danish education planners. Until the late 1970s the codewords in all education were "in-depth study". This went for the Folkeskole, the Gymnasium and all further education. A year more or a year less in a course of study made no difference. A year abroad or 6 months at a Folk High School was considered useful experience. Training as a craftsman and then deciding to become a teacher was a wise move. Being a librarian before going on to university commanded respect. Many medical students had specialised in languages at school and had a year or two's catching-up ahead of them before they could start in medical school.

"In depth and in breadth" – these were the watchwords. It became perfectly normal to meet people trained in one or more branches of commerce but working in a different one. And for some students in-depth studies could last half a lifetime. Either way graduates were well past 40 before they had paid off their student bank loans. The pressure was growing to turn these "eternal students" into temporal beings, and in the 1980s a new Liberal Minister of Education set himself the task of making all courses in Denmark more rational and more efficient. He began by closing a number of Teacher Training Colleges and making university grants dependent on student numbers. Drop-outs or re-sits brought in no cash. University institutes were "slimmed down", particularly in the humanities, medicine and natural sciences.

Reactions differed widely. The more examinations the students passed, the bigger the grant to the university. For a couple of years or so engineers got their degrees on the cheap. Elsewhere teachers elected to go into internal exile and concentrate on their own research, preferably with grants from Danish business – the breweries, medical firms or research professorships set up for the purpose by the Minister himself. This gradually led to research becoming separated from teaching, with the researchers using external grants to buy themselves free from teaching commitments, which junior staff then took over for them.

A third group of teachers chose emigration to foreign universities, either on 1 to 3-year grants (mainly within the humanities) or on permanent contracts (medicine, biology, physics and chemistry). The latter group in particular left, having fired off a fusillade of criticism at the decline of working conditions in Danish universities and the quality of the graduates being produced. Already by the mid-1980s Danish doctors resident in the USA were publicising their opinions, with many prophesying that by the year 2000 there would be too few doctors in Denmark while the rest would be underqualified. Denmark is currently importing doctors from abroad while attempting to repair the damage. The American soldiers were not completely off beam, even if the state of affairs was not quite as bad as they imagined.

Acknowledging the problems

The Minister's efforts were not entirely in vain. In many places university staff had previously done so little teaching that their students considered themselves more or less independent learners. But in particular the cutting of course lengths and the introduction of courses attended and semesters passed as a yardstick for achievement rather than tested knowledge have totally changed the validity and quality of university education. The idea

behind the shortened course that leads to a teaching post in the Gymnasium, to public administration or to commerce and trade has been that the graduate, privately or through further training, should be able to fill in the worst holes and work more purposefully towards employment. For many humanists, however, it has been deeply problematic that for example their knowledge of history or their linguistic ability have been inadequate for teaching in the Gymnasium. Their situation has not been made easier by the fact that on arriving in the Gymnasium they are confronted with a large group of 45 to 55-year-old teachers whose university education in the 1960s and early 1970s was of a higher quality. The many university cuts have resulted in fewer graduates entering the Gymnasium in the last 15 years, where experience-based development has slowed down and the dialogue between older and younger teachers on the subject has had more to do with generation differences than with genuine creativity and quality.

Educational bingo

It was not entirely out of place therefore to call the education situation at the beginning of the 1990s one of shock. Both professionals and civil servants in the system realised that courses in general were not good enough, right through from the Folkeskole to the university. A series of analyses then proved that the policies of the 1980s had been mistaken. Every year, for example, 20,000 youngsters were being refused entry to higher education, mostly on the grounds that their Gymnasium results were not good enough. Angry parents and even grandparents made their objections clear, but all their children could do was to set about gaining extra credits through working in business for a year or two, or attending a Folk High School or taking extra subjects or doing re-sits, after which they might be granted university admission on the Quota 2 basis, set up for those who had not followed the normal path to higher education via the Gymnasium.

To apply for a higher education place thus became something of a lottery – "educational bingo" it was called. A youngster would apply for a place in various institutions for various courses and though successful in one place might turn up at another which had in the meantime become more attractive. It was not a career for life that was being embarked upon, more a taste-and-see trip. For some it was simply an alibi to get the education grant to which all students are entitled.

Those who did get into higher education with high grades from the Gymnasium naturally made tougher demands on their teachers, and soon the sound of hard student criticism meeting soft univeristy chairs was ringing round the country, not least in the form of newspaper feature articles written by students accusing their teachers of classroom incompetence. While largely admitting the problem the institutions could do little about it. A few touched up the story by offering Teacher of the Year awards to popular staff members!

New educational patterns

Yet fluctuating quality and bottleneck entrance problems have nonetheless contributed to the creation of new educational patterns in Denmark. More and more youngsters are choosing to piece together their own education, often through combining a Folk High School course with a higher education course in Denmark and study abroad, an opportunity which has been increased by the "transfer of merit" system now at work throughout the European Union. Danish teachers are less enthusiastic about this than their students.

Furthermore, in recent years the government has been busy creating extra study places for those who otherwise have been applying in vain, and as a result optimism is returning to the field. Teaching institutions are already overcrowded and classrooms in the most popular subjects are bursting at the seams. This does not necessarily entail a drop in quality, for there seems to be no real correlation between the standard of an institution's facilities and the quality of its teaching. Rather it is the students' demand for quality that is a function of the teachers: the demand that teachers should recognize the students' physical and spiritual presence, should teach to a high standard, should be well-prepared and should share planning with the students. At the institutions and university institutes where students have been critical, quality seems to have improved, but where dissatisfied students simply drop out, quality appears to remain low.

Evaluation and innovation

In recognition of the mistakes of the 1980s the Minister of Education set up an evaluation system which for some years now has been analysing and evaluating the quality of a number of institutions. It is doubtful, however, whether it will be a source of innovation and improvement in quality, for with one exception most reports so far simply pat the institutions on the back and send them back to business as usual. It seems instead as if innovation and improvement in quality must therefore be initiated by the youngsters themselves and be supported politically and bureaucratically. Only though combining a critical current from the young with openness and goodwill from the leading politicians is there hope for a good environment for education at the turn of the millennium.

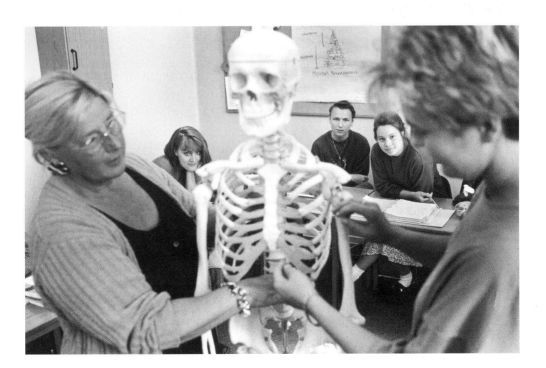

FOLKESKOLE

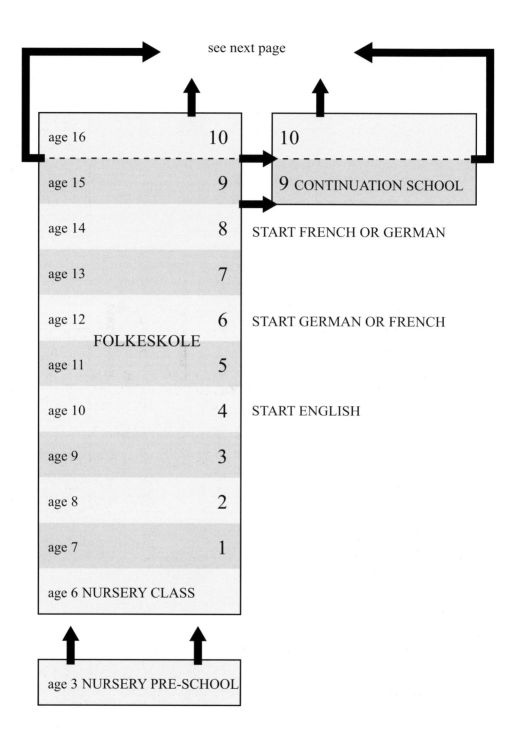

see next page

age 16	10	10
age 15	9	9 CONTINUATION SCHOOL
age 14	8	START FRENCH OR GERMAN
age 13	7	
age 12	6	START GERMAN OR FRENCH
age 11	5	
age 10	4	START ENGLISH
age 9	3	
age 8	2	
age 7	1	
age 6 NURSERY CLASS		

FOLKESKOLE

age 3 NURSERY PRE-SCHOOL

AFTER FOLKESKOLE

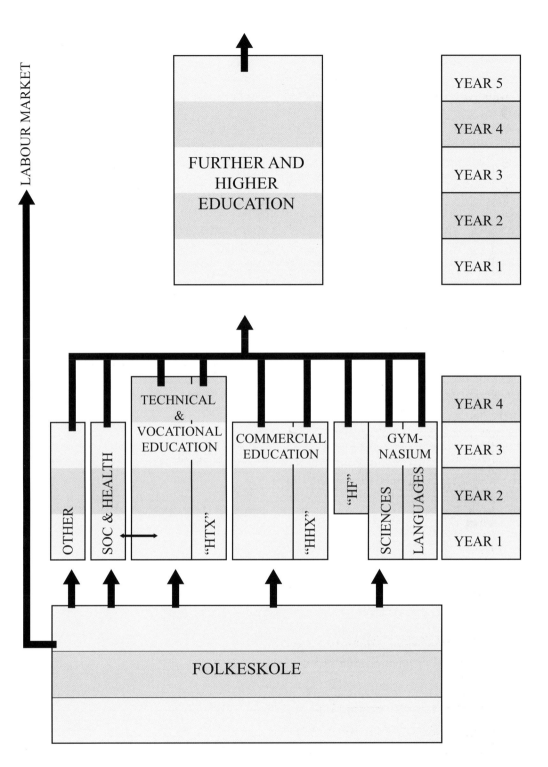

Select Bibliography

Non-fiction

Andersen, Knud Holch: *School Life in Denmark*, Kroghs Forlag, Vejle 1994 (Illustrated book on the Folkeskole)

Borish Steven: *Danish Social Movements in a Time of Global Destabilization: Essays on the Heritage of Reventlow and Grundtvig, The Efterskole, the Postmodern*, Nornesalen Research Center and Kroghs Forlag, Vejle 1996

Borish, Steven: *The Land of the Living: The Danish Folk High Schools and Denmark's Nonviolent Path to Modernization*, Nevada City, CA: Blue Dolphin Publishing, 1991

Danish Ministry of Education: *Dansk-Engelsk uddannelsesterminologi/Danish-English Educational Terminology,* Undervisningsministeriet/Ministry of Education,1995

European Commission: *White Paper on Growth, Competitiveness and Employment – Challenges and Approaches to the 21st Century*, 1994

EURYDICE: *Pre-school and Primary Education in the European Union.* The Education Information Network in the European Union, 1994

Industrial Research and Development Advisory Committee (IRDAC): *Quality and Relevance – the Challenge to European Education, Unlocking Europe's Human Potential*, March 1994

Jensen, Bent Brandt; Nielsen, Mogens; Steenstrup, Jens Erik: *The Danish Folkeskole: Visions and Consequences,* The Danish Council for Educational Development in The Folkeskole, 1992

Jensen, Eva; Sønsthagen, Kari: *Roots in Denmark*, The Danish Ministry of Cultural Affairs and DLIC, 1992

Nordic Council of Ministers: *The Golden Riches of Grass – Lifelong Learning for All,* Nordic Council, 1995

Fiction

Andersen Nexø, Martin: *Pelle the Conqueror vol 1, Childhood, vol 2, Apprenticeship,* Fjord Press, Seattle, USA, 1989 & 1991

Andersen, Benny: *Selected Stories*, Curbstone Press, Willimantic, USA, 1983. *Cosmopolitan in Denmark*, Borgen, Copenhagen, Denmark, 1995

Ditlevsen, Tove: *Early Spring*, Seal Press Feminist, Seattle, USA, 1985

Grundtvig, N.F.S: *A Grundtvig Anthology*, J.Clarke, Cambridge, England, 1984

Hansen, Martin A: *The Liar*, Sun and Moon Press, 1995

Holberg, Ludvig: *Erasmus Montanus*, WITS, Madison, Wisconsin, USA, 1990

Høeg, Peter: *Borderliners*, Harvill Press, London, 1995. *Mirror Image of a Young Man in Balance*, Review of Contemporary Fiction, 1995

Scherfig, Hans: *Stolen Spring*, Fjord Press, Seattle, USA, 1986

Contributors

Foreword. – Per Himmelstrup, Former Secretary-General of the Danish Cultural Institute

Chapter:

1. **Jørgen Carlsen** – Principal of Testrup Folk High School

2. **Agnete Engberg** – Former Chief Inspector of Schools

3. **Bent Brandt Jensen** – Director of Education and Culture, Dragør, Copenhagen
   Kaj Frederiksen – Danish Teacher Union Excutive Committee
   Sidsel & Vinh – Contributors to *The Wednesday Book,* children's diaries for
   April 5th 1995
   Mogens Ballund – Teacher at Brorup School, Skive

4. **Steven Borish** – Research Fellow, Center for Research into Life Enlightenment
   and Cultural Identity, Denmark

5. **Per Schultz Jørgensen** – Professor of Education, Royal Danish School of
   Educational Studies

6. **Hanna Broadbridge** – Paderup Gymnasium, Lecturer in English, Royal Danish
   School of Educational Studies, Skive
   Trine Christensen – Pupil at Aalborghus Gymnasium, Aalborg
   Peter Kuhlman – Principal of Frederiksborg Gymnasium & HF, Hillerød
   Solana Larsen – Pupil at Nørre Gymnasium, Copenhagen

7. **Jutta Rüdiger** – Teacher at Nørre Gymnasium, Copenhagen

8. **Jørgen Carlsen** – see under ch.1

9. **Peder Kjøgx** – Senior.Lecturer and Deputy at Blaagaard College of Education,
   Project Manager, The Danish Cultural Institute, Copenhagen

10. **Peter Bacher** – Director of the Development Centre for General and Adult
    Education

11. **Johannes Nymark** – Principal of Rysensteen Gymnasium, Former Chief Educa-
    tion Officer for the City of Copenhagen

12. **Olav Harsløf** – Director of the Danish State Drama School, Copenhagen

Editorial Board

Hanna Broadbridge – see under ch.6
Ib Fischer Hansen – Principal of Nørre Gymnasium, Copenhagen
Peder Kjøgx – see under ch.9
Edward Broadbridge – (translator) Teacher at Paderup Gymnasium, Randers

Addresses

The Danish Cultural Institute
Kultorvet 2
DK-1175 Copenhagen K
Tel +45 33 13 54 48
Fax +45 33 15 10 91
E-mail: dancult@cultur.dk

The Danish Cultural Institute has offices in 9 European countries: Austria, Belgium, Estonia, Germany, Hungary, Latvia, Lithuania, Poland and Scotland.

Further information about the Danish Cultural Institute and its departments abroad can be found on the Internet under **Kulturnet Danmark, http://www.kulturnet.dk.homes/dki**

Denmark's homepage on the Internet is at: http://www.danmark.dk
This contains addresses, phonenumbers and links to almost all other Internet addresses, including public ministries, steering organs, boards and committees etc. as well as a number of NGOs with links to various homepages.

The Danish Ministry of Education
Frederiksholms Kanal 25
DK-1220 Copenhagen K

The Danish Council for Adult Education
International Secretariat
Loengangstraede 37
DK-1468 Copenhagen K

The Folk High Schools' Information Office
Vartov
Farvergade 27G
DK-1463 Copenhagen K

The Folk Day High Schools' Information Office
Herskabsvejen 1
DK-4800 Nykoebing F

Center for Research into Life Enlightenment and Cultural Identity
(Nornesalen), Ollerup
5762 Vester Skerninge, Denmark
Fax +45 62 24 28 66.

The Danish Teachers Union
Vandkunsten 12
DK-1467 Copenhagen
Tel +45 33 69 63 00
Fax +45 33 14 11 94

The Danish Gymnasium Teachers Union
Lyngbyvej 32
DK-2100 Copenhagen Ø

The Vocational Teachers Institute (SEL)
Thomas B. Thriges Gade 48
DK-5000 Odense C

Terminology

For a fuller terminology see
Dansk-engelsk uddannelsesterminologi (Ministry of Education 1995)

13-scale. Most Danish examinations are marked on a scale of zero to 13, where zero to 5 is failed, 8 is national average, 11 is distinction and 13 is quite outstanding.

adult education: voksenuddannelse (18+)
adult education centre: voksenuddannelsescenter (VUC)
adviser: konsulent
agricultural school: landbrugsskole (20+)
BA/BSc: bachelor (3 to 4-year course)
basic education: basisuddannelse
courses for unskilled and upgraded workers: arbejdsmarkedsuddannelse (AMU) for ufaglærte og tillærte
day-care: dagpleje
day-care centre: daginstitution
general education: almendannelse
Commercial school: handelsskole (16+19)
comprehensive school: folkeskole (6-15)
computer science: edb lære
Continuation school: efterskole/ungdomsskole (15-16)
county: amt(s-)
county centre for educational materials: amtscentralen for undervisningsmidler
County high school: gymnasium (16-19)
Craft school: håndværkerskole
distance teaching: fjernundervisning
district council: (land-)kommune
Domestic school: husholdningsskole
doctorate: doktorgrad
education association: oplysningsforbund
educational counsellor: studievejleder
educational theory and practice: pædagogik
Evening school: aftenhøjskole
examination syllabus: eksamenspensum
executive order: bekendtgørelse
Folk High School: folkehøjskole/højskole(16+)
further/higher education: videregående uddannelse
head teacher of Folkeskole: skoleinspektør
head teacher of Gymnasium/HF: rektor
High school: gymnasium
high school teacher: gymnasielærer ("adjunkt" for 15 years, then "lektor")
individually organised youth education: den fri ungdomsuddannelse (FUU)
leaving certificate: eksamensbevis
leaving examination: afgangseksamen
MA/MSc: cand.mag/scient (NB. the Danish Master's Degree is higher)
mark/grade: karakter

Ministry of Education and Research: Undervisningsministeriet
mixed ability grouping: undervisningsdifferentering
municipality: (by-)kommune
nursery: børnehave
nursery/pre-school class (in the Folkeskole): børnehaveklasse
part-time education: deltidsuddannelse
Popular Educational Association: Folkeligt Oplysningsforbund (FOF)
practical training: erhvervspraktik
pre-school teacher: børnehavepædagog
Production school: produktionsskole (16+)
progressive free school: lilleskole
registered childminder: dagplejemor
remedial teaching: specialundervisning
report (official): betænkning
Royal Danish School of Educational Studies: Danmarks Lærerhøjskole (DLH)
scholarship/grant: stipendium
school board of governors: skolebestyrelse
special class (for slow learners): hjælpeklasse
supply teacher: vikar
teacher: lærer
teacher training college: lærerseminarium
teaching of immigrants: indvandrerundervisning
Technical school: teknisk skole (16-18)
Trade school (EUC): erhvervsskole (16-18)
vocational basic training: erhvervsgrunduddannelse (EGU)
vocational courses: erhvervsmæssige kurser
Workers' Educational Association: Arbejdernes Oplysningsforbund(AOF)
Youth school: ungdomsskole

Index